PUNCHY'S HAMPSHIRE YEARS

PUNCHY'S HAMPSHIRE YEARS

Cricket and Dancing

Alan Rayment

with Stephen Chalke

Foreword by
Reverend Canon Timothy Biles

CHARLCOMBE BOOKS

This book is dedicated to
Love and Laughter
both greatly valued by Alan

Text © Alan Rayment, Stephen Chalke & Timothy Biles

The photographs in this book are from Alan Rayment's collection

The following works have been consulted and occasionally quoted from:
Dave Allen, *Hampshire County Cricketers* (Moyhill Publishing, 2018)
John Arlott, *Days at the Cricket* (Longmans, Green & Co, 1951)
Arthur Conan Doyle, *A Reminiscence of Cricket* (1900)
Arthur Conan Doyle, *The Story of Spedegue's Dropper* (Strand, 1928)
Len Hutton, *Fifty Years in Cricket* (Stanley Paul, 1984)
Colin Ingleby-Mackenzie, *Many A Slip* (Oldbourne Book Co, 1962)
Roy Marshall, *Test Outcast* (Pelham Books, 1970)
David Matthews, *Derek Shackleton – On The Spot* (Blackberry Downs, 1998)

Charlcombe Books
e-mail: stephen.chalke@hotmail.co.uk
tel: 07968 138122

First published 2021

ISBN: 978 1 7399293 0 5

Printed and bound in Great Britain by
CPI Antony Rowe, Bumpers Way, Chippenham SN14 6LH

Contents

	Special thanks	6
	Foreword by Reverend Canon Timothy Biles	7
	Uncertainty	9
	Introduction	11
1	From Lord's to Southampton *1945 – 1949*	19
2	Happy in Hampshire *Summer 1949*	35
3	A lifelong friendship *Tim Biles*	61
4	Books, cows and nappies *Winter 1949/50*	65
5	Who will bat at number three? *Summer 1950*	73
6	Farm, family and dancing *Winter 1950/51*	90
7	A fateful stroll around the ground *Summer 1951 and Winter 1951/52*	94
8	Connections *Meditating on a conversation in 1951*	106
9	Four summers of county cricket *1952 – 1955*	118
10	Living life to the full *A successful dancing business*	130
11	Cricket every day *1956 – 1957*	141
12	The tremendous mystery *November 1957*	153
13	Into the unknown *1958*	161
14	A summer at Lord's *1959*	173
15	Later life	182
	Index	190

Alan, Elizabeth Lloyd and Tim Biles

Special thanks

In putting together this book from the writings and papers left by Alan, I am most grateful for the help I have received from a number of people. First among these is Elizabeth Lloyd, who did so much for Alan in his last years and has been determined that his labours on this book would not be in vain. Her support for the project has been crucial to its completion.

Dave Allen, the Hampshire County Cricket Club archivist, spent several years encouraging Alan to get this book written, and he has provided me with excellent notes on the county's cricket during Alan's years. Tim Biles, Alan's oldest friend, has offered much encouragement as well as a beautifully written foreword. Alison Barnes, Alan's niece, was a helpful and perceptive reader of the final text. Andrew Bradstock, biographer of David Sheppard, contributed valuable insights, as did the Reverend Malcolm Lorimer, who gave me a greater understanding of Alan's spiritual experiences as they would have been viewed by theologians in the 1950s.

It cannot be the book exactly as Alan would have written it, but I hope that between us we have created something that is true to what he set out to write.

Stephen Chalke

Foreword
by Reverend Canon Timothy Biles

It was Easter 1949, and I was one of many young lads – then aged 13 – being coached by the Hampshire professionals in the nets at Southampton's County Ground. Mr Gerry Hill was encouraging me with underarm lobs which I usually missed. In the next net a dashing young man was smashing the ball with such power that I asked Mr Hill, "Is that man Denis Compton?"

"No," said Mr Hill. "That's our new batsman, Mr Rayment."

"Wow! We'll win the Championship," was my response. So I can claim to be Alan Rayment's first fan.

Little could anyone have guessed that within a year I would be godfather to Denis, his first born, and that seventy-two years later I would officiate at his funeral. The star-struck fan had become a life-long friend.

Alan's early years in wartime Britain had been very traditional. He had been baptised in the Church of England, he had sung in the parish church choir and learnt the Anglican tradition so well that he even went to his bishop offering for ordination to the priesthood. But soon other traditions and cultures were challenging his Anglican roots. He was drawn to Eastern thinkers and to the theories of reincarnation among Hindus and Buddhists, and he was attracted by the openness of the Quakers who encouraged free thinkers. But they required silence in worship and Alan was always a great talker and wanted to sing, so that didn't last long. The search went on, undefined and unfulfilled, but his love of life continued and wonder at the whole creation never ceased to grow.

His letters to me – and I expect to others – always ended wishing me *'love and laughter'*. Those words – his words – sum up the man I knew. He looked at life with love and laughter. He aspired to create love and laughter. He wished love and laughter on the world. Love and laughter eliminate judgement and negativity, and he had no time for either. Love always bubbles over into laughter.

Alan, for all his searching in the exotic East, was a much more orthodox Christian than he realised. He may have ignored many rules and traditions, but he was close to the heart of what matters. *'God is love and those who live in love, live in God,'* says St John in one of the Epistles. And that was

Alan's aspiration. Maybe this wasn't quite the temperament required in the professional game. And we never did win the Championship in his playing days!

It is now a matter of great joy that the noted cricket writer Stephen Chalke has gathered together all the papers that Alan was working on in his later years and has produced a record of his ten Hampshire years and of the adventures and misadventures of the years that followed. He has done it with the same warmth and sensitivity that was the hallmark of Alan's life, and I trust readers will reflect on those times sensitively, with renewed love and laughter.

*Alan with his infectious smile and his familiar cravat
– with Dave Allen, Hampshire CCC archivist*

Uncertainty

This passage was almost the last written by Alan

NOW, on the first Monday of October 2020, the majority of our fellow human beings are experiencing a high level of uncertainty about sustainable life on Planet Earth. Of the many realities that inflame our uncertainties, global warming, population growth and the demolition of Nature's biodiversity are powerful destructive forces that will inevitably cause the extinction of Life on Planet Earth and therefore our own demise.

Who is responsible? US! You and me. Our species – millions and millions of US – are blindly constructing our own extinction!

NOW is a time of heightened UNCERTAINTY! Nature's warning sirens, the Covid19 viruses, are wailing night and day in every human community throughout this world. Will our intelligent species listen and learn, grow up and act in time to reverse our downhill rush to self-extinction and climb the hills and mountains to reach wisdom and maturity and sanity – TO LIVE LIFE IN HARMONY WITH MOTHER NATURE AND REALLY LOVE OUR NEIGHBOURS AS OURSELVES?

Since February this year the coronavirus pandemic has extinguished over one million lives. In many nations around the world medical services and supplies are stretched to the limit. Large corporate pharmaceutical companies and major university medical research departments are focused on creating and testing a viable vaccine to counter the spread of the virus; national economies are in danger of collapsing, and unthinkable numbers of people are now unemployed. Also unthinkable is the fact that in a majority of countries a minority of people gather in small and large crowds, ignoring official rules and common sense about wearing face-masks and 'social distancing'.

Global warming, environmental damage and population growth are tangible realities to many people around the world who study those subjects, visit problem locations or devote their lives to research and practical change or campaigning. Many other people maintain a serious interest through modern media and literature. However, the plethora of information available has not yet made sufficient impact on enough people to energise a world-wide awakening and radical change.

The alternative? Homo sapiens, and all creatures great and small, are heading towards extinction!

*

Having written the above piece, I decided to record the trailer to Sir David Attenborough's latest film-documentary which Elizabeth and I watched on television last evening, October 8. Sir David is the doyen of all natural historians, the most prolific in producing film-documentaries about the wonders of nature on our planet and the effects of our human management of its resources, both good and ill.

A LIFE ON OUR PLANET

I am David Attenborough, and I am ninety-three. I've had the most extraordinary life – it's only now that I appreciate how extraordinary. The living world is a unique and spectacular marvel, yet the way we humans live on earth is sending it into a decline. Human beings have overrun the world. We are replacing the wild with the tame.

This film is my witness statement and my vision for the future, the story of how we came to make this our greatest mistake. How, if we act now, we can yet put it right.

Our planet is heading for disaster: we need to learn how to work with nature rather than against it. And I am going to tell you how.

*

NOW, October 2020, is also a time of personal uncertainty regarding the completion of this book. Given the history of recent fluctuations of my respiratory and urological health I have not been able to give the time or focus to research and writing that I was able to give in the first six months of 2019. I may, therefore, need to change my writing style, change gear and speed up the story.

As with my first book of memoirs, *Punchy Through The Covers*, I am writing my story for my children, grandchildren and future generations of their families, also for friends and a few cricket enthusiasts. My hope and expectation is that I will complete the draft chapters for this book by the spring of 2021.

Alan died in hospital on Tuesday 27 October 2020

Introduction

Alan's first book, *Punchy Through the Covers*, was published in the summer of 2013, when Alan was 85 years old. A tour de force of personal memory and social history, the 384-page book covered the first 21 years of his life from his North London birth to the twin joys of marrying Betty, his childhood sweetheart, and becoming a professional cricketer with Hampshire. The plan was for this to be the first of three volumes: the second to cover his years in cricket and dance, the third his remarkably varied later life.

My first contact with Alan came six years earlier, in January 2007, when he rang for advice about publishing. By this time I had been writing and publishing books about cricket for ten years, many of them set in the era in which Alan played, but I can only recall one occasion when his name had cropped up in my conversations with former players.

"Hampshire had a chap called Alan Rayment," Gloucestershire's 'Bomber' Wells said to me one day. "He was the nicest man I ever played against. He always had a smile on his face."

Alan had already been writing his autobiography for some years, and he wanted to know how many words were in an average book. I am a great believer that books should be whatever length is natural for them but, trying to be helpful, I ventured the figure of 100,000. When he said that he had written 70,000, I was initially reasured.

"And have you nearly finished?" I asked.

"Oh, no," he replied. "I've only reached the age of 17" – at which point he told me that he was yet to write about his ten different careers. He listed several of them – social worker, estate agent, psychotherapist, dance studio proprietor – and I became most intrigued. Two days later I was driving down from Bath to Milford on Sea, south of the New Forest. If nothing else, I figured, he would make a good subject for my monthly article, *The Way It Was*, in *The Wisden Cricketer*.

Longcliffe, where he lived, was a large, gabled, inter-war building full of old-fashioned character, a home in its day for a family of substantial means. It was split into five flats, in the attic one of which Alan lived on his own. It was far from spacious, but Alan had made it cosy and we settled to a conversation that started before 10.30 and was still going strong seven hours later. I say 'conversation', but mostly Alan did the talking, which suited me fine.

He was full of laughter and of stories, which he interspersed with strikingly fresh observations about life and people. Happy to open up about spiritual matters and sexuality, with seemingly nothing off limits, he was quite different from any other cricketer I had interviewed.

We talked about his years as a dance instructor. Mark Ramprakash, the England cricketer, had just won the fourth series of *Strictly Come Dancing*, following in the footsteps of another cricketer, Darren Gough, who had won the previous year. "I am in awe of how those teachers get the celebrities up to that standard," he purred with enthusiasm, "plus all the hard work the celebrities put in."

He talked with insight about the similarities between cricket and dancing – the physical co-ordination, the discipline – and I was spellbound. As a dance teacher he had developed an eye for the distinctive movement of a person. "If Marilyn Monroe walked past," he said, "I wouldn't be looking at her figure. I would be taking in how she walked. It's a trained observation, not something I'm conscious of until I think about it."

He was on his feet in the flat, comparing two great bowlers of his playing days, Derek Shackleton and Fred Trueman. "To me Shack was Fred Astaire, up here, light on his feet, beautifully balanced, while Freddie was Gene Kelly, a totally different technique, down here with his knees bent."

My own Hampshire hero from those years was Roy Marshall, the white West Indian who opened the batting so thrillingly. "There was a Caucasian stiffness about Roy," Alan said, "as well as a relaxed, born-and-raised-in-the-sunshine movement. He was wonderfully co-ordinated but, combined with the looseness, he had a slightly military stature and walk."

Jimmy Gray, Marshall's opening partner? "He could make a very good dancer, but his mindset isn't towards it." And Henry Horton, the stalwart number three in those years? "No. If Roy was a racehorse, Henry was a carthorse. Big-boned, slow-moving. He had farmworkers in his genes."

Playfully I asked him to visualise cricketers of more recent times, and he entered into the spirit of it with an exhilarating freedom of thought.

Flintoff had "too yeoman a build", Vaughan "could be good if he let his innate reservations go", Monty Panesar "has got it, but he would have to stand up straight", Pietersen "could be a very good Latin American dancer, but he hasn't got the total discipline for a ballroom dancer. He would find the foxtrot and the waltz boring."

On and on he went, as I continued to feed him names. Shane Warne? "He would fit the showbiz, Hollywood, razzamatazz side of the American version. I don't see him doing it on British television, though." He stopped for a second: "I'm just thinking on my feet, Stephen."

We finished with David Gower – "He had everything. The beautiful co-ordination, the grace, the timing, the nonchalance, the sophistication. He would be the very best, and I don't think he would be embarrassed" – and Ian Botham: "No, he'd be hopeless. I don't think he'd even begin. I don't think he'd want to."

I cannot convey to you the joy I had listening to him. He was a breath of fresh air, seeing them all for what they were, unique human beings. As the great West Indian cricketer Everton Weekes once said to 'Bomber' Wells, "Everybody walks differently."

I was writing a book with Tom Cartwright, the former England cricketer whom many considered the best coach in the country and who, alienated from the establishment, was working with youngsters in deepest Wales. I told him of my conversation with Alan, and he was in rapture. "He's looking at them as individuals, isn't he? He's starting from their natural movements. That's what we've completely lost from English cricket. He's not trying to make them fit into some perfect biomechanical template."

The day after my visit to his flat, Alan rang me twice. 'I think he's going to loom large in my life for a while,' I noted in my diary, 'and I don't mind that. He has such a strong life force, and he has caught my imagination.' I wrote the article, and I was pleased with it. It was something different.

I offered to help him with the publishing side of his autobiography when he was ready, but I sensed – correctly – that that was some way off.

Two years later I met him for lunch at Drusilla's Inn, a pub down a narrow country lane in Dorset, when I got him to tell me in full detail the extraordinary story of his summer as a coach at Lord's. That, too, became an article in *The Wisden Cricketer*. He reported back with amusement how everybody at the Hampshire Old Players' Reunion, even the current players, were commenting on how often he was bobbing up in the magazine.

He became a regular member of the Dorset Cricket Society, which meets every Thursday afternoon in winter. With such an extensive programme to fill, I gave a talk to them most years, and always Alan was sitting cheerfully in the front row, spreading a positive energy that lifted the spirits of all those around him. Often he rang after a meeting to tell me about other speakers: which ones had stimulated him and which had little sense of giving of themselves to an audience. He was fascinated by people, as I am, and his observations were rich with revealing insights, often distinct from

Alan, at the age of 78, having a bowl after a Dorset Cricket Society meeting

what other people might comment on. After one of my speeches, to my great pleasure, he complimented me on my breathing technique.

Our telephone conversations became a part of my life, and they were never dull or depressing. There was always a sparkle, a liveliness, a curiosity about life, even in his moments of adversity.

His book progressed, in fits and starts. Eventually in early 2013, six years after our first meeting and goodness knows how many years after starting it, he completed it to his satisfaction. I laid it out for him, I proof-read and indexed it, and he re-read it with great care, making sure that every sentence was how he wanted it. I introduced him to my printers, and in early June the copies were delivered to Longcliffe.

At the same time I was publishing a new book by John Barclay, the former Sussex cricketer, and that same day I collected the copies of that from the printers. I arranged to meet John for a celebratory pot of tea at the Grosvenor Hotel in Stockbridge, where we were joined by the former cricket correspondent of *The Times* John Woodcock, who had written the foreword to John's book. Then Alan turned up with his book, accompanied by his son Stephen. We were all hard at work, signing books and talking, when a large party filled the bar.

"Alan Rayment?" exclaimed one man, catching sight of the book. "He's not here, is he?" He turned out to be a cousin whom Alan had not seen for many years. The first sale was made.

It was an exciting time for Alan, and he was keen to get cracking on volume two. Yet, alas, his progress was slow. In the words of the Preface that he wrote in January 2019, 'Good intentions drafted a few chapters as I drifted through months and years of lazy wellness.'

Perhaps the effort of writing the first volume had taken too much out of him, and the prospect of undertaking two more such books was too daunting. Perhaps the years were slowing him down. And perhaps he did not feel the need to revisit his cricketing years as strongly as he had those of his childhood and adolescence.

When he turned 90 in May 2018 his companion Elizabeth, who gave him so much support in his last years, organised a surprise lunch, attended by his friends from the cricket world. There were about sixty of us, and we gathered at the Mayfair Hotel in Bournemouth, sitting expectantly at the tables ahead of Alan's arrival. Elizabeth had told him that they had tickets for a Bournemouth Sinfonia concert, and he arrived at the hotel, thinking they were stopping for a quick sandwich. When he walked towards the room, a voice called out, "Ladies and gentlemen, please rise for Mister Alan Rayment" and we all stood up and clapped. It was a magical moment.

Special guest was Mike Barnard who, back in the 1950s, had spent his winters playing at inside-left for his home town, Portsmouth, in football's old Division One and his summers batting alongside Alan for Hampshire. By this time they were almost the last survivors of the Hampshire team of those years but, while Alan remained in remarkably good health, Mike was frail in a wheelchair, never having recovered fully from horrific injuries sustained in a coach crash almost fifty years previously, injuries that he had borne steadfastly without complaint or self-pity. Alan called him "the most courageous man I have ever known".

Speeches followed lunch. Dave Allen, the Hampshire archivist, recalled highlights of Alan's cricket career and presented him with a large jigsaw based on a photograph of Alan himself. "It's the perfect image for anyone attempting to account for and explain the life of Alan Rayment, the man with so many interests and achievements," he said. "Put them all together in the correct pattern, and you have a picture of a man who is still with us, surely because he loves life so well." Or, as a woman friend in California once told Alan, "I know you're a Gemini, Al. I reckon there's at least fourteen of you."

Alan's impromptu speech in response was superb, saying the right things with eloquence and great warmth, sending us home with a glow in our hearts.

Five years had passed since the publication of *Punchy Through the Covers*, and inevitably the occasion prompted questions about volume two. This spurred Alan into fresh activity. 'Occasionally and slowly,' he wrote in his preface, 'I began the long task of sorting and filing archived research material, journals and memorabilia stuffed randomly in boxes and drawers.'

He was troubled by the patchiness of his memory, and he reflected on this in the preface. Moments of great emotional importance remained clear, but so much else had disappeared completely from his consciousness. Perhaps he was making his task harder by trying to write chronologically about his cricket, printing out old scorecards in the hope that ancient incidents would resurface in his mind. He might have done better to follow the flow of what he could recall. I had a plan to spend time with him, guide him in that direction, but I was busy. Then, when I was ready, Covid struck and we could not meet. Though he was 92 by then and needing supplementary oxygen, he was still full of life whenever he rang. I thought he had more time than he did.

His preface contains a passage of reflection about the nature of memory, ending with the promise of further exploration of this in volume three:

That which I term my 'emotional memory' is still deep and clear. By that I mean moments that were recorded within my brain's limbic systems through sight, sound, touch, feel, emotions, instincts, patterns, environments, circumstances and experiences.

For instance, in my first book I was able to recall, with ease, the scenes, the sounds, the smells and the 'feel' of the occasion when watching the maiden voyage of the ocean liner RMS Queen Mary in May 1936, two days before my eighth birthday:

> I was with my parents and cousins among a crowd of excited adults and children on Puckpool beach near Ryde on the Isle of Wight when, after waiting impatiently for a very long time, a few dots appeared on the western horizon of The Solent, grew nearer and larger until the huge flotilla of ships, yachts and pleasure craft attending The Queen Mary – an enormous, glisteningly beautiful ship with three symbolic funnels and 'dressed overall' – sailed slowly and majestically past our cheering and waving crowd – then slowly faded into the distant horizon by the Nab Tower.

From my cricket I have an internal 'video' of the scene at the United Services ground in May 1952 when I drove Somerset's Bertie Buse for the four runs that notched my maiden first-class hundred:

> I 'see' the curved run-up of his non-athletic body melding into his rhythmical text-book action; I 'sense' my concentration, 'see' the ball – a medium-paced out-swinger coming towards me – 'see and sense' myself shaping for the cover drive and placing the ball through the gap to the left of extra cover … the bat over my shoulder in the follow-through … then eyes on umpire George Mobey as he signals 'four' to the scorers.

End of video.

Eagle-eyed readers will notice later in this book that the four took him to 99 and that he completed his century with a single. But in a sense that supports Alan's point about 'emotional memory'. His mind had preserved the essence of the occasion, the emotional details that mattered.

BUT I have NO recall of moments, people, scenes, scores or incidents – or even playing – in eighty-plus percent of my 199 first-class matches, few when twelfth man and even fewer of the second eleven matches for the Hampshire Club. Similarly, in all other aspects of daily life I am blessed with heightened recall of a small percentage of scenes, events and people across a wide range of life experiences – then a blank disc on everything else.

However, as is normal with the majority of people who write personal memoirs, the act of writing stimulates recall and memories, some short and vivid, others long and surprisingly detailed – they 'pop up from somewhere' and cause us to exclaim, "Where on earth did that come from?" Although only applied to one event in this book, I have experienced recall of past events in this life through psychological techniques – and regression into past lives: but all that in the next book … if I live to 100?? That long??

Alan died in October 2020, at the age of 92, leaving barely half of what he had intended to write in this volume two – and nothing of volume three.

He started this volume two with some brief passages from volume one, describing how he came to play for Hampshire, but the fresh writing spanned only the years from 1949 to 1951, plus some powerful and very personal chapters about his religious awakening and his retirement from cricket in 1958. In addition there were files full of notes, scorecards, photographs and various articles.

How best were we to proceed? Elizabeth, Dave Allen, his great friend Tim Biles and I discussed the options. We decided that I should write up his story as best I could, using his written testimony where it exists, adding in passages from taped conversations and rounding it out where necessary from other sources. It cannot be the book that Alan would have written if he had had time, but it should still capture some of the essence of what he wanted to say about his years of cricket and dancing.

His funeral, attended by a Covid-restricted congregation of only thirty but watched online by many more, was conducted by Canon Tim Biles, who knew Alan longer than anybody in the cricket world. Beautifully he captured the essence of Alan's spiritual journey through all the adventures of his life, and he has expanded this address as the foreword to this book.

I hope that we have done justice to Alan in this book, both for those readers who knew him and enjoyed the stimulation of his uplifting company and for those who did not have that pleasure. He was a special man.

1

Lord's to Southampton

1945 – 1949

Perhaps our story should begin on a warm, bright morning in April 1945. The sixteen-year-old Alan had left school the previous summer and, with his examinations passed, was working in an office for Unilever. His parents were, in his words, "on the lowest rung of the middle class" – his father a commercial traveller in the rag trade, his mother a dressmaker and pianist – and Alan's dreams were all of being a cricketer, playing every day of the week. With the encouragement of two senior clubmen at Finchley, Alan's parents had paid for him to attend the Easter coaching classes at Lord's.

> Dressed smartly in grey suit, white shirt and Finchley club tie, I walked with light step and brimming heart along the tree-lined Litchfield Grove, carrying my long leather cricket bag to the bus stop at Church End.
>
> My feelings were mixed: calm yet excited, apprehensive about arriving at St John's Wood. What would it be like at Lord's ... *Lord's*! ... I'm going to bat and bowl at Lord's. I wonder who will be my coach – who I will meet – what will the other boys be like – mostly from public schools, I expect. Thankfully, I was a socially confident teenager, used to mixing with men and boys from posh backgrounds in the middle-class environment of London club cricket. Most of my excitement was focused on what I might learn – how much I could improve my skills – and which famous county players I would meet at the nets.

Happily Alan's coach for the week was a benevolent North Londoner, Frank Lee, who opened the batting for Somerset and who, in time, would become one of the game's leading umpires.

> More than any of the high points of my life up to April 1945, that week in the nets at Lord's was the mountain peak – and Mr Lee my shamanic guide. Under his wise, quiet-mannered tutelage, my batting technique improved enormously. I was a hard-hitting young batsman with an attacking temperament, blessed with quick

footwork and fast hands. I scored most of my runs by powerful front-foot drives on both sides of the wicket, square cuts and pulls. But my defence was weak, especially on the back foot. Frank Lee transformed my back-foot play, both defence and attack, drilling into me the mantra, "Back and across – back and across – eyes in line with the ball – watch the ball all the way!" He himself was a builder of innings, and he talked to me about that.

By the middle of the week my defensive play was tighter, though still vulnerable due to my attacking temperament and desire to hit the ball out of the net – which I did, often. More than one pulled drive disappeared over the groundsman's sheds and beyond the wall into Wellington Road. "Don't hit too many," he said at one point. "We can't afford losing the balls."

I became aware that the head coach, Archie Fowler, was having a chat with Frank at the bowler's end, after which Mr Lee strolled down the wicket to have a quiet word in my ear: "Hit 'em hard but keep 'em down, young Alan." Wonderful coach, wonderful man, Frank Lee: always patient, soft-voiced and wise, never discouraging ... the best!

I was further encouraged later in the week by the increasing numbers of spectators who gathered behind my net when I was batting. I was still only sixteen and somewhat naive about the significance of this development until Frank Lee took me aside and said: "Some of the 'big wigs' were watching you yesterday, and again today, Alan."

"What do you mean, Mr Lee ... what are 'big wigs'?"

"Now don't let this go to your head, young man, but Sir Pelham and Mr Robins – and even the Colonel – were all watching you today. Mr Robins came round the nets to ask me who you were and where you are from – and if you become good enough to play first-class cricket when you are older, whether you would play as an amateur or a professional."

"Did he really?" I replied, surprised and embarrassed, knowing that Mr RWV Robins had captained Middlesex before the war and had played for England. "I don't know what to say, Mr Lee ... and who is the Colonel?"

"The Secretary of the MCC, Colonel Rait Kerr," was the reply. "We don't often see him out here ... you go off now to eat your sandwiches and I'll talk to you again this afternoon" ... leaving me in suspense with lots of questions racing around in my mind.

What a summer it was for Alan. On the recommendation of a Finchley club veteran, he was attending dance classes. "You have naturally quick footwork," the man told him, "but you could improve if you learned ballroom dancing. Jack Hobbs and Charles Fry, both great batsmen, were accomplished ballroom dancers."

At their first class he and his mate Pete Sutherland felt uncomfortable and embarrassed, with Pete only lasting one more session. But for Alan it was a life-changing experience.

> My attitude to female dance partners changed, embarrassment faded, confidence increased and skills developed until I was able to complete a circuit of the dance floor in the waltz and quickstep, even mastering the natural spin turn in both dances. In those few weeks I discovered that I really enjoyed this dancing lark.
>
> It was fun meeting up with several old school friends, boys and girls, but there was not a thought or a whiff of romance for many weeks. I danced with Iris Cramphorn, even dared to hold hands as I walked her home, but there was no real romance in my life ... *until!*
>
> Pete reported for training as a naval cadet at Chatham. He had been 'walking out' on a regular basis with the lithesome brunette, Betty Griffin. He asked me to look after Betty until he came home on his first leave. Two weeks later Iris and I decided to meet at Betty's house and chaperone her to the Saturday dance. I do not remember why, but a heated argument ensued which resulted in Iris storming off home and Betty and I going on to the dance. In that brief moment of time a dramatic and unexpected change of partners determined our future pathways for a long time – a lifetime, in fact.

Adding to the joys of that summer, the war ended – in Europe in May, in the Far East in August – and Alan's cricket blossomed. Recommended by Frank Lee, he was selected in June to travel to South Wales to play two matches for a London Counties side, the first against a Glamorgan XI at Newport.

> It was my first invitation to play in a team with well-known county players, my first long-distance train journey to play cricket, my first stay in a hotel and my first game on a ground where county cricket had been played.

Added to the felicitous joy of this occasion was the identity of his London Counties captain: Joe Hulme, the former Arsenal and England footballer and Middlesex cricketer. In April Alan, a promising footballer, had played in the winning team in the final of the North Middlesex Six-a-Side Tournament, a match that had been refereed by Hulme, who was now the Tottenham manager. After the game Hulme had taken Alan aside and recruited him to play the next winter for the Spurs' junior side. Doors were opening for Alan, and the trip to Wales was another.

> Rationing was tight, travel restricted and wages low. The prospect of a seventeen-year-old travelling with seasoned professional cricketers and veteran amateurs from London to Newport to play cricket was, at that moment, beyond my comprehension.
>
> That summer I sailed along in a breeze of naive self belief, combined with the sunshine of enjoyment. I truly loved playing, improving, meeting new people and climbing the lower rungs of the ladder of success.

In August Alan played three matches at Lord's: a two-day game for the Air Training Corps against the Royal Naval College, a rain-ruined game for Sir Pelham Warner's Lord's XI against the Forty Club, and finally – most memorably – for a Colts XI against the Cross Arrows.

This last game, for the Middlesex Colts, took place the day after the final day of a match between England and The Dominions, which Alan watched as a spectator and considered to be 'the greatest cricket match I have ever witnessed'. Played in the best of spirits, it featured two centuries by Wally Hammond, some spectacular hitting by Keith Miller and the last first-class appearance of the great West Indian Learie Constantine, accorded by his team-mates the honour of leading the Dominions after their captain Lindsay Hassett pulled out before the match.

> I felt both exhilarated and exhausted as I queued for the bus back to Finchley where I overwhelmed my parents, during and after supper, with dramatic stories of the day. Tired and happy I went to bed early, knowing I would be returning to Lord's the next day. Having experienced cricketing paradise, what gifts – sweet or sour – would the morrow bring?

The next day would prove to be one of the great days of Alan's cricketing life. Captained by Walter Robins, with the former England captain Gubby Allen standing as umpire, the Middlesex Colts were under the spotlight and they did not disappoint in the field, dismissing their opponents for 174. What followed remained fresh in Alan's mind for the remaining 75 years of his life, a dream-like episode at the end of a summer of joy.

Sir Pelham Warner's Lord's XI, 1945
Back (from left): Unknown, Ian Bedford, Alan Ratcliffe, D O'Shea,
Michael Fitzgerald, E Murphy, John Stacey, Alan Rayment
Front: Bill Wignall, Sir Pelham Warner, Ronnie Aird, Archie Fowler, Jim Sims

Our opening pair played themselves in against the Middlesex fast bowler Laurie Gray and the medium pace of the veteran Lord's pro Bill Wignall, then played themselves in again against accurate spin bowlers, skilfully protecting their wickets but adding so few runs to the total ... a definite 'dawdle'.

Next to bat, I was sitting on the balcony watching the action – or inaction – when I became aware that Mr Robins was pacing up and down in the dressing room, firing off questions to members of the team: "Do those batsmen always score so slowly? ... We need runs on the board ... Do they think we're playing for a draw?"

Seconds later Walter Robins, small in stature but bristling with the energy of frustration, was standing next to me on the balcony, hands cupped around his mouth and shouting: "*HIT OUT OR BLOODY WELL GET OUT!! ... DO YOU HEAR ME, BATSMEN? ... HIT OUT OR BLOODY WELL GET OUT!!*"

His angry energy reverberated through my body, firing off my own adrenaline … because, silently, I agreed with him. "Well, I'll soon be in," I thought as I returned to the dressing room to gather my gloves and bat, swing my arms and legs to warm up – and to do something with the nervous energy pulsing through my body and brain. "I'll attack the bowling, pinch singles. Yes, I'll have a go – and if I get out quickly, Mr Robins will see that I tried to move the score along."

My team-mates at the wicket were trying but failing, another four overs producing only eleven runs. Our angry captain went out on the balcony again: "BATSMEN … ONE OF YOU GET OUT … GET RUN OUT … WE NEED SEVEN AN OVER!"

About three hundred boozers and sober aficionados standing around the concourse in front of the old Tavern could hear every word, especially as the wicket was close to the Tavern boundary. The most inebriated took their cue from the famous England player and began to barrack the batsmen. A sardonic cheer greeted a desperate slog, resulting in splayed stumps. I was in!

Walter Robins placed his hand on my shoulder: "I don't mind if you get out quickly, Rayment. I do mind if you and the other batsmen do not make a big effort to win this match. Good luck."

Alan got off the mark, then found himself on strike against the returning Laurie Gray, coming down the slope from the pavilion end. Here was the moment of truth, and he flashed a square cut for four, then nicked a ball past second slip for another four.

We knew nothing of 'the zone' in those days, but for the rest of that innings I experienced 'that otherness' for the first time, therefore recall only a few scenes in my video memory. I lofted an off-drive one bounce into the pavilion and pulled a six over the short boundary into the Tavern boozers, followed by the winning pull shot for four to the same boundary. Eighty not out – game won with time to spare.

Laurie Gray and his team-mates congratulated me as we walked towards the pavilion gate; Taverners clapped and cheered; a sprinkling of MCC members nodded and muttered 'well done' as I walked up the steps and through the Long Room where I was met by a beaming Walter Robins: "You won the game for me – and your team, young Rayment. Splendid innings, one you'll always remember. Thank you – well played!" Praise indeed.

> At Lord's, when seventeen, I played one of the best innings of my life – an innings that opened the door to all that was to follow in my cricket career.

*

In June 1946, now turned eighteen, Alan made his debut for Middlesex 2nd XI at Hove, scoring 18 and 4 and 'beginning to understand the jump from good club cricket to the standard of county second eleven games'. More special in his memory was the game the following Sunday when he was selected to play for Gubby Allen's XI against Southgate Cricket Club. Not only was he captained by his first cricketing hero, Patsy Hendren, but he batted before tea with his second hero, Denis Compton.

> Although I had talent and was 'promising', I realised I would never be in the same league as Denis Compton. But I thoroughly enjoyed the experience and remember chatting amicably with my hero as we walked off the field, both undefeated and having put on an unbroken stand of 59.
>
> After tea I again felt as proud as Punch as I followed Patsy Hendren onto the field of play. I remember his chirpy voice saying, "Out to the covers, young Alan, I expect a couple of run-outs from you."

Two years of National Service began during that summer, disturbing the progress of Alan's cricket. Recruited into the RAF, he undertook his initial training in Cheshire.

> Cockroaches invade my first memory-picture of the square-bashing camp. To snapshots of cockroaches infesting the kitchen of the Airmen's Mess, add the horrible taste of bromide in the tea, the prickly woollen underwear, a sore neck from the barber's clippers, our fascist hut corporal – and you will gather, dear reader, that we were not at a Butlin's holiday camp. And SHINE! – everything had to shine to perfection and beam a reflection to shave by ... be polished, scrubbed, pressed, immaculately folded and stacked before inspection – or painted white. So there was some truth in the old joke: 'If it moves, salute it; if it don't, paint it.'

The 'fascist' corporal was responsible for passing on to Alan a telegram.

> "Yer've gotta telegram, Rayment. I 'ope it's not bad news, but in case it is I want yer to open it an' tell me who sent it and what it says."

"Yes, Corporal," thinking he had a bloody cheek to demand knowledge of something that was obviously a private matter. I slit open the small buff envelope and read the following:

SELECTED MIDDX II V SURREY II OVAL AUG 24/26 STOP ALSO CAPTAIN MIDDX YA V SURREY YA OVAL AUG 31/SEPT 2 STOP CONFIRM AVAILABILITY STOP SIGNED G.O ALLEN LORD'S STOP

Two Stripes, staring intensely into my eyes saw my face light up with surprised excitement rather than sadness as expected. He shouted, "Well, no-one 'as died then. Tell me what it bloody says, Rayment."

"I think you'd better read the telegram, Corporal."

An eternity of silent seconds passed before the explosion. Shaking with anger, he waved the telegram in front of my face, exclaiming: "What the fuckin' 'ell do you think this place is ... a bloody holiday camp ... cricket ... bleedin' ponces' game ... you're confined to camp for six weeks, Rayment ... tell this bloody Allen bloke that ..."

"Excuse me, Corporal, but Mr Allen is a famous captain of England, and I think the commanding officer should see this telegram. Should I put in a written request for an interview with the CO?"

My calm response and mention of 'written request' to the CO stunned Two Stripes into open-mouthed speechlessness until, realising he needed to 'save face' in front of his charges, he gulped and turned towards the door, exclaiming: "I'll 'ave to talk to the sergeant about this bleedin' telegram, Rayment." Then glancing back, he jabbed his right arm and index finger at our silent groups, yelling "And yer lot of pale-faced wankers, get on with the bloody bull!"

In the 2nd XI match, playing under the captaincy of Gubby Allen, Alan scored 0 and 37. Against the Surrey Young Amateurs he hit 33 and 25, facing the bowling of 'a small, rotund, thirteen-year-old boy who bowled high-flighted leg-spinners, expensively'. His name was Colin Cowdrey.

Alan's memory was sharper when it came to the aftermath back at the camp. Arriving at his hut at 3 a.m., clutching his cricket bag, his attempt to grope his way to his bed led to his knocking into the stove, dislodging it from its stack pipe and, unbeknown to him as he slept, filling the room with soot. When he woke, he was confronted by an apopleptic corporal, who set in motion a charge that led to his having to report to the squadron-leader's office. The outcome was not what the corporal had anticipated.

"Rayment, my dear chap, I hear you have had an unfortunate accident ... something to do with your cricket bag and a stove. Are you all right? ... Now tell me – what it was like playing at The Oval ... I read that you scored a few for the Young Amateurs ... and that Gubby Allen himself captained your second eleven."

Thirty minutes later I left the CO's office having recounted details of both matches, the players involved and the 'feel' of playing at The Oval. As I was going through the door the CO called out: "Oh, by the way, Rayment, we're having net practice this evening. Do come over and join us – meet the chaps – get to know them – because, as I said, you'll be skippering the team tomorrow."

As a result of this episode the hated corporal was relieved of his position at the hut, adding to Alan's popularity among his fellow servicemen.

*

In 1947 Alan represented Combined Services against Northamptonshire, a first-class match, being bowled for 5 in his only innings. Then in June 1948, stationed at Uxbridge and able to live at home, he was summoned to play for Middlesex 2nd XI against Hampshire at Dean Park, Bournemouth.

We stayed in a pleasant, moderately priced family hotel at Purewell, Christchurch. After dinner Tommy Dewhurst and I took a stroll to find the River Avon. We were surprised by the quaint bridges and adjoining ruins of the ancient monastery. Always sensitive to new environments, I felt strangely at home, as I did the next morning when we arrived at Dean Park.

The beautiful playing area was almost circular in shape, surrounded by pine trees and large Victorian residences with a cosy pavilion built in a similar style to the houses. I noticed a strange low level building twenty yards from the pavilion – a long shed with a rounded roof rather like a railway carriage. On enquiry I was told that the shed had been the professionals' changing rooms before the war when only the amateurs used the pavilion dressing rooms.

Little did he know it, but his innings of 40, battling patiently against the left-arm spinner Reg Dare on a turning wicket, was to change his life.

In August, out in the Arden Field of his beloved Finchley Cricket Club, he watched as the Hampshire Chairman, Mr WK Pearce, arrived at the ground, walked 'impolitely' in front of the members' enclosure and climbed the steps into the pavilion for a meeting he had arranged with the top brass of the club, including Alan's mentor Cyril Harvey. He had also arranged to speak to Alan's parents.

> I was not consulted because legally, at the age of twenty, I was still a 'minor'. I was quite cross about this antiquated and undemocratic process. I knew next to nothing about the Hampshire club and had many questions I wished to ask. Burned into my emotional memory of that day is the condescending manner in which the Hampshire chairman addressed a few guarded words to me before he left.
>
> Cyril Harvey was a civil servant of liberal mind and cheerful manner who lived opposite our house. The next time we met I questioned him about the meeting with Mr Pearce. Cyril emphasised that the discussion went well and there was a strong possibility I would be offered a two-year professional contract. He then surprised me with a remark that drilled itself into my memory: "Alan, some of us are worried about your future because if you do sign as a professional you will then become working-class."

Alan's dream had always been to play for Middlesex at Lord's, and this unexpected turn of events confused him. His first thought was to seek out Frank Lee for advice, but Lee, now an umpire, was standing in a match at Taunton. So instead, with that get-up-and-go spirit that he never lost, he opted to track down Patsy Hendren, the idol of his early cricket-watching days and now the coach at Sussex. Armed with sandwiches made by his mother, he caught a fast train from Waterloo to Brighton, took a taxi to the ground and arrived before lunch on the second day of a match against Yorkshire.

> Mr Hendren ushered me to a quiet spot in the pavilion and listened attentively to my story. He answered my questions about Hampshire cricket and named a number of pre-war players who would soon retire. He also pointed out that Desmond Eagar was keen on building a young team of talented players.
>
> I then asked a rather cheeky but serious question: "Do you think there is any possibility of joining the Sussex staff, Mr Hendren?"
>
> He laughed and said that the county already had a crop of very good young players waiting their opportunity to play in the first team. He gave me no definitive advice, but our discussion had cleared my head. If offered a contract, I would sign for Hampshire.

The letter from Desmond Eagar duly arrived, offering a two-year contract. Immediately Alan's life took two great steps forward. He and Betty arranged to get married in October, and he accepted Hampshire's offer, albeit with two conditions: (i) that the county would help to find them suitable accommodation, and (ii) that they would arrange interviews with him for work in the winters.

> Mr Eagar replied to my letter saying the Committee agreed to those requests and that the two-year contract from 30 March 1949 carried a year-round wage of five pounds per week, less a deduction of four shillings and eleven pence for the National Insurance stamp. Small bonuses included expenses of £1–10s home and £3 away for first-team matches and £3 for a win. Talent money for exceptional performances applied to first-class matches only. All travel and hotel expenses were paid by the County Club when playing for official Hampshire teams.
>
> I wrote again to Mr Eagar, enclosing a letter of consent from my father, accepting the terms of the contract and stating I would be available to sign the documents in Southampton while on honeymoon in Bournemouth.

A great new adventure lay ahead of Alan, and it began on Saturday 23 October 1948, the day of his wedding.

> I remember dressing soon after dawn – bursting with happiness – my mind busy with the list of things to do, yet reflecting for a moment that I was leaving my parents' home and starting a new phase of life with new responsibilities in a new place. It was as though we were disembarking from an ocean-going family yacht into an eight-foot sailing dinghy intent on reaching an island just visible on the horizon in uncertain weather conditions.
>
> Thankfully the weather was sunny and warm. As Betty and I knelt at the altar for prayers pronounced by the Rector, I felt a gentle loving 'presence' hovering above my right shoulder – an invisible personal benevolent energy that remained in place through the prayers to the end of the Benediction.
>
> Also readily retrieved from my mind-film-sound memory are the symbolic and romantic scenes of the reception and 'going away' including the tuneful buzz of happy chatter swirling among young friends and older relatives which changed key to 'ooo's and 'ah's of admiration when Betty rejoined the guests in an unforgettable 'going away' outfit.

Wedding day

They stayed at the Cumberland Court Hotel in West Cliff Gardens, Bournemouth, now a block of flats.

The hall porter carried our suitcases to Room 23, my significant number, and returned with a light meal and a pot of tea on a large tray. With no experience and little information, love-making was a passionate learning curve from virgin naivety to athletic success. Hand in hand, we explored Bournemouth's beautifully landscaped central gardens, the pier, the beach and western promenade leading to Alum Chine. We discovered Fisherman's Walk in Boscombe where I carved a heart, arrow and initials 'A-B' on a tree; we laughed our way to Swanage on a smoky steam train, strolled awhile along the promenade until spray from rough seas made us dive into a greasy-spoon café; showed off our dancing skills on the perfect sprung floor at Bournemouth's Pavilion and cuddled up in the back row of the Odeon cinema to watch Moira Shearer and Robert Helpmann dance in the film 'Red Shoes'.

On Wednesday, as arranged, they caught the train to Southampton Central station where they were met by Arthur Holt, the Hampshire coach, who proceeded to take them on a tour of the city in his new Morris Minor Traveller, a tour that ended at the docks where he presented a pass to the guards and they entered a world which captivated the ever-inquisitive Alan and Betty.

A world of huge ships and cranes, of little steam engines shunting railway stock, of big lorries being loaded and unloaded and hundreds of busy dock-workers animating the mechanical cacophony. To walk the length of the RMS Queen Mary in dry dock was the highlight of an unforgettable experience. Arthur certainly charmed Betty and me long before we entered the gates of the Hampshire County Cricket Club's headquarters in Northlands Road.

At the ground Arthur Holt led them to a small outer-office where they were introduced to Mr Pearce, the Chairman, and to the Secretary and captain, Desmond Eagar. Alan was impressed by the framed photographs of old Hampshire teams that lined the wall, Betty was at ease joing in the light-hearted pleasantries, and the four of them settled to the formal discussion in the Secretary's office, with Eagar setting out his vision for the club.

"We're building a new team, Alan – a mix of older experienced players and younger ones with talent and potential. Every team member *must* be a good fielder! Hampshire are going to be the best fielding side in the Championship."

His enthusiasm and dynamic energy reminded me of my RAF skipper, Alan Shirreff. *Wisden* records that they played against each other in the Varsity match of 1939, also that Alan had played a few games for Hampshire under Desmond Eagar's captaincy. I politely mentioned the fact that I had enjoyed playing for RAF teams captained by the Squadron Leader.

The only other topics of conversation that I remember were my concern about the cost of accommodation in Southampton and employment during the off-season. The Hampshire captain and chairman assured me and Betty that they would recommend suitable accommodation early in the New Year and ask members of the committee to suggest potential opportunities for employment during the close season of 1949/50. Thus reassured, I signed both copies of the two-year contract and thanked the three men of Hampshire for the opportunity to develop my abilities and, hopefully, to achieve my ambition to become a county cricketer.

The affable Arthur Holt drove us to the railway station, wished us well and waved as our 'Battle of Britain' class 4-6-2 engine pulled away, emitting clouds of steam as though celebrating the signing of two contracts in one week: 'Marriage and Hampshire CCC'. The new Mr and Mrs celebrated with a jig in the empty carriage, then cuddled up in the corner to enjoy the autumnal New Forest landscape unfolding through the screen of the window frame – symbolising the unfolding of our dreams towards the reality of fulfilment.

During their first winter of marriage Alan and Betty remained in London. Betty began teaching ballroom dancing classes two evenings a week, and in the New Year she became pregnant, with the baby expected in October. Meanwhile they saved money in preparation for their move to Southampton, surprising Alan's father with their financial diligence. Unfortunately there was no such diligence shown by Hampshire County Cricket Club who, by the end of February, had sent them no accommodation details.

Desmond Eagar, embarrassed and apologetic, agreed to arrange for copies of Southampton's *Daily Echo* to be mailed to our address. Betty and I responded to several advertisements by telephone and made an appointment for a viewing at 22 Burgess Road the next Sunday, March 6.

On that cool bright morning we were in high spirits when we alighted from the steam train at Southampton, excited by the prospect of inspecting a potential home near the County Ground and a bus ride away from the sea. Having purchased a local street map at the station we decided that it would be pleasant to walk up The Avenue beside The Common to Burgess Road – pleasant, yes, but three miles was further than we estimated. Passing the Cowherds Inn we joked about being Fred and Judy – Astaire and Garland – who had performed a famous musical number in the recent film 'Easter Parade':

> *We're a couple of swells, we stop at the best hotels,*
> *But we prefer the country far away from the city smells ...*
>
> *The Vanderbilts have asked us up for tea,*
> *We don't know how to get there, no siree ...*
>
> *We would drive up The Avenue but we haven't got the price,*
> *We would skate up The Avenue but there isn't any ice,*
> *We would ride on a bicycle but we haven't got a bike,*
> *So we'll walk up The Avenue,*
> *Yes we'll walk up The Avenue,*
> *And to walk up The Avenue's what we like.*

For a few moments we skipped along, hand in hand, singing:
> *Yes, we'll walk up The Avenue 'til we're there.*

Number 22 Burgess Road was a small detached house squeezed between the pavement and the northern boundary of The Common. The owners, Mr and Mrs Dear, were a pleasant and polite couple in their late forties who, having welcomed us warmly, became reluctant to accept us as tenants when we shared the news of a baby due in October. I proposed a compromise, saying that, because I had to report to the county club in three weeks' time, would they agree to letting the two rooms until we had settled in our new environment? We would then seek other accommodation in June or July. Thankfully they agreed; we agreed to pay two pounds ten shillings per week for the two furnished rooms with shared use of the kitchen and bathroom.

Back in Finchley, Betty and I gave due notice to employers and landlady. Our parents, never openly emotional, wished us 'all the luck in the world': my brother Derek, now twelve and playing football at the County School, gave me a hug and said he looked forward to seeing me play at Lord's. Bob Holmes, a new friend who was a pupil at Betty's dance classes, offered to drive us to Southampton.

So on Saturday 26 March we squeezed our essential possessions in Bob's Austin 10, weaved our way past familiar North London landmarks – Golders Green, Swiss Cottage, Lord's and Hyde Park, across the Thames – then through the unfamiliar South London conurbation to Guildford, over the Hog's Back, round Winchester's pre-war by-pass to arrive in Southampton three and a half hours later.

Alan Rayment in May 1949

2

Happy in Hampshire
Summer 1949

Alan and Betty had three days to fill before he reported to the County Ground, and they passed them happily: taking a train to the nearest beach at Netley, visiting Mayes' department store which was celebrating the end of clothes rationing, discovering with surprise the trams in the High Street and walking boldly into the Guildhall to admire the magnificent dance floor. Then on Wednesday Alan caught the bus down Hill Lane, walked briskly through The Cut and entered the gates of the County Ground in Northlands Road. He reported to the Assistant Secretary, Dick Court, who introduced him to a group of capped players.

Patsy Hendren was right about the age of the Hampshire team. The county had ten capped players: two amateurs, Desmond Eagar and Charlie Knott, and eight professionals, five of whom – Johnny Arnold, Neil McCorkell, Jim Bailey, Lofty Herman and Gerry Hill – were old enough to have played under Lord Tennyson almost twenty years earlier. Even the other three – George Heath, Neville Rogers and Gilbert Dawson – were more than ten years older than Alan. In their company Alan's bubbly self-confidence gave way to an embarrassed shyness. Then Arthur Holt led him to the room for the uncapped players at the east end of the Ladies' Stand..

> We entered a small dark and rather scruffy room, known as The Black Hole, in which a group of young players were chatting, smoking and laughing. Arthur introduced me to Jimmy Gray who, when he could get a word in over the volume of raucous banter, named names, some of whom shook hands with me. All were outwardly friendly, but those who spoke in broad provincial accents seemed wary of my relatively posh London tones and traditional manners.
> Another newcomer, six-feet-five at the age of fifteen, Malcolm Heath from Walton-on-Thames, also sounded a bit 'plummy'. In contrast the other newcomer, with a distinct regional accent, was Cliff Walker, a 29-year-old Yorkshire businessman from Huddersfield who had played five first-class games for his county

but not gained a regular place. Although Cliff was a director of a chain of family cinemas and could afford to drive a new Jaguar, he had decided to sign professional forms with Hampshire.

Half an hour later Arthur Holt popped his head inside the door of The Black Hole and yelled, "QUIET!" He announced that all twelve of us were to join the capped veterans in their dressing room. Accessed by an open staircase adjacent to the playing arena, The Hutch was a small changing room and balcony perched above the mower shed beside the Members' Stand.

Now overcrowded with a vociferous bunch of professional cricketers, Desmond Eagar delayed his pre-season talk because there was one absentee. When veterans Jim Bailey and Lofty Herman called out "He's coming, Skipper", all eyes turned to the window overlooking the playing area to watch a small man with fair wavy hair, splayed feet and a rolling gait stroll across the cricket square towards the stairs of The Hutch. Johnny Arnold, Hampshire's leading batsman, double international and senior professional, was greeted with a burst of high-spirited banter. 'Obviously a popular character,' I thought to myself.

The Skipper began to speak enthusiastically about his expectations for the coming season. With tact and diplomacy he referred to the fact that some of the younger players had a great opportunity to establish places in the team because several of the veterans would soon be retiring. He also emphasised that one of his priorities was to build the best fielding team in the Championship.

Arthur Holt then outlined the pre-season arrangements. For the next week and a half there would be two hours of nets in the morning, followed in the afternoon by physical training, six-a-side soccer and fielding practice. The following fortnight would see them all running Easter coaching classes for the sons of members. Then, in the run-up to the first match on Saturday 7 May, there would be four two-day practice matches.

I revelled in every aspect of the pre-season programme. I discovered holes in my defence when batting in the nets against Derek Shackleton and Charlie Knott, noted that my seam bowling was played with nonchalant ease by Johnny Arnold and Neville Rogers but that I was quicker and more accurate than anyone in ground fielding and throwing skills – except wicket-keeper Leo

Harrison who was also a superb outfielder. The soccer was fun and competitive, the PE minimal and almost laughable. I was already fit and became marginally fitter.

I felt accepted by the uncapped pros and realised I had had the experience of adjusting to so many individual and team personalities in the previous four seasons – though mostly in an amateur setting. Now there was a hint of professional competitiveness and the likelihood that some of us would not progress to a regular place in the championship team. I was thankful for my two-year contract.

After the schedule for the Easter Coaching Classes was announced, I was taken aside by Desmond Eagar and formally introduced to Neil McCorkell, with whom I was paired to travel to Portsmouth. Neil, who made his debut in 1932, was in the top echelon of first-class wicketkeeper-batsmen, a quiet, thoughtful family man soaked in cricket experience and worldly wisdom. He became my first mentor in this new world of Hampshire cricket.

I thoroughly enjoyed coaching the boys aged between eleven and sixteen. I had the privilege of watching a fifteen-year-old boy, Michael Barnard, being coached by Neil in the adjacent net. Michael was an outstanding batsman and amazing fielder for his age. I learned that he also excelled at rugby and soccer.

Net practice intensified during the last week in April, followed by an Under versus Over-30s game, a seriously competitive affair for the twelve uncapped professionals: John Taylor, Jim Gray, Ralph Prouton, Reg Dare, Leo Harrison, Derek Shackleton, Harold Dawson, Tom Dean, Dick Carty, Malcolm Heath, Cliff Walker and myself. Four uncapped amateurs were also available: David Blake, Reverend John Bridger, Vic Ransom and David Guard. Who among the Black Hole inmates might show good enough form to be selected for the first few championship matches – even to replace one of the ten capped players, who if fit would almost certainly play the first matches?

I was enjoying every moment on and off the field, bursting with energy and confidence. The banter between all the players was friendly, similar to that experienced in the Finchley Club and RAF dressing rooms. Friendships were developing with Cliff Walker and his wife Marion, with Jimmy Gray and Ralph Prouton, both of whom were local ex-grammar school boys and promising soccer players.

> Jimmy surprised me one day with an unanswerable question: "Alan, where do you get your confidence from?" Cycling home, I asked myself: "Do I have a 'high and mighty' attitude? Am I cocky or talk too much? I don't think so. In fact, I am quite shy in some respects – though I like people and get on well with most types. I do exude a confident energy because I am fit and happy, married and playing cricket, enjoying this way of life, especially when comparing today against working in that gloomy office in London. Why should happiness and confidence be a problem to any of my colleagues?"

Alan played in two of the practice matches. For the Under-30s he batted and fielded well, hitting a fifty in one innings. Then, in a 2nd XI fixture against Gloucestershire at Northlands Road, he scored an impressive 45, sharing in a century partnership with fellow newcomer Cliff Walker. Arthur Holt and Gerry Hill complimented him when he came off, and at the end of the game on Thursday he was told to report to Desmond Eagar in his office.

> The Skipper's beaming smile signalled that he was in a good mood, but I did not expect the very firm handshake accompanied by the words, "Congratulations, Alan, you have been selected for the first six championship matches. You will report here tomorrow at 10 a.m. to board the coach for Cardiff. It is a long journey so, although lunch is arranged, I suggest you pack some sandwiches. I am delighted that the selectors are giving you this early opportunity to gain experience as a batsman. Actually, your brilliant fielding and enthusiasm tipped the scales.

There was, however, a sting in the tail. In the second innings against Gloucestershire he had been dismissed for 16, deceived by a slower ball from a young Arthur Milton. Taught at Finchley to come off with a smile on his face at all times, he returned to the pavilion looking the picture of happy contentment. This was clearly not to the liking of Desmond Eagar.

> "I have to reprimand you about a matter brought to my attention by the senior professionals. They cannot understand why you smile all the way back to the pavilion when you get out for a low score. Remember, Alan, you are no longer an amateur club cricketer or playing for the RAF with Alan Shirreff's chaps and their 'jolly good show' attitude. Of course I want you to enjoy your cricket with Hampshire, but cricket is now your job and, as a professional, has to be taken more seriously."

What was it that they had said to Alan at Finchley? "Some of us are worried about your future. If you sign as a professional you will become working-class." It all raced round his head as he made his way home that afternoon.

> Gee, what an opportunity! I'm thrilled and determined to do my utmost best for the team – and myself. But why do those friendly old pros think I'm not serious when playing cricket? Of course I'm serious when doing any job. Doing a job properly is part of who I am, as intrinsic as saying 'please' and 'thank you'. Was I not serious when I made that billiard table – or sang in the choir – or studied for the dance teacher's exams – or asked Betty to marry me? And am I not seriously happy that Betty is pregnant? But there is serious and *serious*. That our country might have been invaded by the Nazis was *serious* – as was the Blitz and the horrendous loss of life in the war. Those wartime events were *seriously unhappy* – the consequences, too. Oh my! Life gets complicated sometimes.
>
> I jumped off my bike and ran indoors to give Betty a swinging hug – round and round with her feet off the floor while babbling away with my news: "I'm off to Cardiff tomorrow … in the first team for six Championship matches … playing first-class cricket … against so many famous players … It's really happening for me, for us, Betty my love."
>
> We were seriously happy!

Nicknames are part of the initiation into sporting teams, and Alan soon acquired his: Punchy – as one dictionary has it, 'lively spirited and vigorous'.

> Maybe the cheerful personality of this London Kid presented something of a puzzle to those friendly old Hampshire pros in 1949 – at that time 'old' being a relative term for cricketers over 35.
>
>> "Well, he's a mixture. He's well-mannered but not a prude, He's got the voice and confidence of an educated Londoner and three initials too, but he's not an amateur or posh. He plays football, he's married, his wife's having a baby, and he's a bleedin' dance teacher – I thought all dance teachers were poofters! And he's brilliantly 'nuts' at cover with a hell-of-a-throw to the keeper. You know what? He's bleedin' Punchy!"
>
> The nickname stuck: a title that identified me in the cricketing world through ten seasons with Hampshire and continues to be used today

> among family, friends and cricketers. Thank you, you dear 'old pro' friends of yore, for the nickname that stuck. A moniker that befits my Geminian personality – I think?

Next morning, as he waited for the bus to the ground, thoughts tumbled around his excited mind.

> Selected to play in the first six County Championship matches; so unexpected – such a surprise; so soon – such an honour; so inexperienced – I hope I score fifty. Am I really travelling to Cardiff today? The Skipper said to bring some sandwiches. Do I have pyjamas in this suitcase? Is this really real?

At the ground a 1930s Albion motor coach awaited them. There was a jovial buzz of early-season excitement as the burly driver, assisted by Len Sprankling, the county's diminutive scorer, loaded the bags into the luggage hold, then they were away – rumbling slowly through the winding roads of Wiltshire and Somerset before stopping for a pub lunch near Gloucester. With no Severn Bridge, it was a seven-hour journey, which ended at a hotel near the Cardiff Arms Park ground.

Alan shared a room with fellow debutant Cliff Walker, rising early to relax in the warm water of an antiquated bath. Once more the thoughts ran round his head.

> Happy thoughts of Finchley's Arden Field; of watching Hendren, Compton and Constantine at Lord's; of Frank Lee and the 'big wigs' looking at me in the nets, of all those who had encouraged and supported me.
>
> Then came the anxious thoughts. Will I become a good enough batsman to win a regular place in the Hampshire team? And now that I am a professional, will my love of the game slip downhill because I am supposed to put on an act of being *seriously anxious*?
>
> I doubted that playing cricket every summer's day would cause me to be less happy – more likely inspire my youthful energies to overflow with cheerfulness. Unless ... unless I fell out of favour with those veteran professionals.

It was Saturday 7 May 1949, and only two of that Hampshire eleven had been born later than 1919: Alan and the 20-year-old David Guard, an amateur who had played for the county three years earlier while still at Winchester College but had not yet lived up to his schoolboy promise.

Notably absent from the young professionals selected was the 24-year-old Derek Shackleton, who a year earlier had arrived from Yorkshire as a leg-spinning all-rounder. One day in the nets, desperate to find another opening bowler, the county had asked everybody to bowl with pace. "Even Desmond tried to bowl fast," Alan remembered being told. "He was like a gander, running up, all arms." Shack was the chosen one, and he showed great promise when he played in the first team as a medium-quick bowler. So why was he not in the side to go to Cardiff?

> Rumours circulated that 'they', the selectors, thought he had become swollen-headed due to his success last season.
>
> Really? Shack swollen-headed? Not then, not ever, could Derek Shackleton's personality be tainted with that characterisation. The wise and modest Gerry Hill shared his opinion with me that some members of the committee had seriously misjudged Derek's character.

Through the three days of the match Glamorgan, champions in 1948, held the upper hand. A stylish century by Gilbert Parkhouse set up a total of 337, and Hampshire were struggling to avoid the follow-on till David Guard, in the highest score of his short first-class career, batted resolutely for 89. On the last day the visitors were set for 276 for victory but, after the fall of early wickets, they settled for a draw, ending on 180 for five. Alan, down at number eight, batted in the first innings only.

> I remember little about my debut match except that off-spinner Len Muncer bowled me 'through the gate' for 2 and that, in the absence of 'Shack', Gerry Hill's slow-medium seamers were inadequate support for veteran George Heath. Fielding at cover point was a joy, the melodious tones of Welsh voices joyful.
>
> We boarded Old Albion soon after six o'clock on Tuesday evening, paused at Glouccster for fish and chips – for some a pint – chatted or dozed or played cards. Disembarking from the coach just before midnight, we scattered to our homes. Desmond Eagar, driving a Wolseley, gave me a lift to Burgess Road on his way home to Bassett.
>
> At breakfast the next morning Betty and I shared her news and my experience of the journey to Cardiff, the game and the players. She unwrapped my gift of a brass jug purchased in the Welsh capital; then we decided that we could no longer afford souvenirs when I played away games, as I had when with the RAF and Middlesex 2nd teams. No more brass to clean!

With a three-day break before the next fixture there was time for Alan to ask the senior pro, Jim Bailey, how to close 'the gate' with the bat-pad forward defensive technique.

> I find it interesting that I knew nothing of that essential technique, either through observation or the little coaching I had received.
>
> Jim Bailey – rotund raconteur, urbane prize-winning snooker player and an intelligent, friendly cricket professional – showed me how to slide the top hand round to the back of the bat handle, extend the left arm and, importantly, keep the blade just in front of or beside the left pad and slant it at an angle – hands well in front of the toe of the bat. I adopted that technique immediately.
>
> But why did I have to ask? Why had I never discussed 'grips' with anyone? At the age of thirteen I had studied Don Bradman's batting in the *Daily Mail* book of sequential photos of each shot, but I do not remember studying his grip. I had been coached by the delightful Frank Lee, Alf Gover, Andy Sandham and Dennis Hendren. I had played with and against many county and several ex-England players, all friendly and encouraging people. But 'variety of grips' was never a topic of conversation.
>
> During the season of 1949 and halfway through the next I studied the grips of many batsmen. Prolific run-scoring batsmen Jack Robertson and John Langridge placed the top hand in the old-fashioned Jack Hobbs manner, the wrist over the top of the handle and the thumb-index finger V in line with the front of the bat's shoulder. Harold Gimblett's V lined up between the bat's shoulder and rear of the splice; Len Hutton's V pointed further round, almost beyond the splice. I clearly remember changing my basic grip in June 1950 to a position similar to that of Harold Gimblett.

After that break it was off to The Oval to play Surrey, runners-up in 1948. Alan, again at number eight, scored 23, taking part in a stand of 61 with skipper Desmond Eagar. But Hampshire had to bat second time on a rain-damaged pitch and were unable to cope with the bowling of Jim Laker and Alec Bedser. All out for 59 – Rayment stumped McIntyre bowled Laker 0.

> We lost by an innings and 58 runs, arrived back in Southampton early evening, dispersed to our homes in good time for an early supper – and for me to iron cricket shirts and trousers in preparation for the match next day against Nottinghamshire. My home debut.

Hampshire at The Oval, May 1949
Standing: Neville Rogers, Alan Rayment, Cliff Walker, Neil McCorkell,
George Heath, Jimmy Gray (twelfth man), Gerry Hill
Seated: Jim Bailey, Charlie Knott, Desmond Eagar, Vic Ransom, David Guard

A Wednesday morning at the County Ground. Alan's first appearance in front of Hampshire's supporters. He reconstructed the occasion in his mind seventy years later, imagining himself on the players' balcony, looking down at a scene that would become a familiar part of his life:

> Groundsman Ernie Knights tending the green-brown wicket in the midst of the light-emerald outfield, a promising flow of paying spectators passing through the Hulse Road turnstiles and hurrying to their favoured viewpoint on uncomfortable planks supported by four tiers of timber framing that encircled two-thirds of the playing area.
>
> Below and to my left, scores of club members chatting in pairs and casual groups, some strolling on the grass in front of the

picturesque Edwardian pavilion, a few sipping an early ale in the shade of the upper tier. The majority of men dressed in blazers or sports coats and the obligatory club tie, most of the ladies in tasteful tailored or floral frocks and low-heel shoes, a few sporting straw hats or colourful headscarves.

Derek Shackleton was back, but his bowling in the match consisted of only three overs in Nottinghamshire's first innings and two in the second.

Had the selectors decided that Shack needed to be nursed? Laughable! Had Bailey and Knott influenced Desmond Eagar in order to protect their potential annual haul of wickets? Maybe. Did the non-selection episode and being snubbed in this match negatively affect Derek's quiet composure and confidence? Absolutely not!

Hampshire, batting first, got off to a good start with a faultless, four-hour century by Neil McCorkell.

I remember his exit because, secretly, I was cross with the partner who ran him out. What do I remember of my own experience? Answer: 'the old pros of Nottinghamshire'.

The visitors were older even than Hampshire, three of them in their forties: captain Bill Sime and openers Wally Keeton and Charlie Harris. It was 240 for five, well into the evening session, when Alan arrived at the crease.

I got off the mark, nudging a few singles from the pace bowling of Frank Woodhead before pulling the left-arm spin of Bill Sime for four along the turf, the ball going through the plank stands into the nursery ground.

Change of bowler. Charlie Harris from the pavilion end. The old pro. He made his debut with Nottinghamshire in 1928, the year I was born. He was renowned as a comedian and prankster, a talented yet eccentric batsman who, on a whim, would decide to play shots for twenty minutes, then block every ball for the next twenty whatever the state of the game. Now aged 41, he opened the batting and bowled off-spinners. The 20-year-old 'Kid from North London' was about to encounter the wily, wizened, wisecracking, hard-nut veteran professional all-rounder from 'Up North' – near coalmines and factory chimneys!

Jim Bailey was on strike, pushing Harris's second ball for a single. I took guard and checked the field placings, having noted that those two balls were slow and flighty. My first ball I played defensively, the ball rolled slowly down the pitch to Harris who picked it up, took a long hard look at me and returned to his run-up marker. His next delivery was a slow, loopy half volley which I drove, following through from my high back-lift. A hush, then the crashing sound of broken tiles on the roof of the Ladies Stand. Sustained clapping. Umpire Harry Parks raised both arms aloft ... Six!

Charlie Harris walked slowly ... very slowly ... down the pitch towards me, furrowed brow on serious face inches from mine. He stared into my eyes.

"Yoooung man, is thee t'amateur?"

"No, Mr Harris, a professional with three initials."

"Well, thee's got a blooody cheek to 'it t'senior professional over 'is 'ead for six!! Watch thee don't do it again, yoooung man!"

My emotions were mixed: thrilled that I had timed that fluent drive so perfectly; surprised that Charlie Harris had questioned my status; chuckling about his order 'don't do it again'; a mental note that his next ball would be a 'tempter' ... which it was! The pace was slow and the flight so high I had time to debate my options ... forward defence or ... wait, wait and drive the ball for another six?

Decision: a Jim Bailey coached, exaggeratedly stylish bat-pad forward defensive stroke ... left leg fully extended to line of flight, reverse grip of left hand round the back of the handle, left arm straightened to create a thirty-degree angle for the bat placed, with 'soft hands', slightly in front of my padded left leg. Result: 'dead ball' right under my nose. Charlie Harris strolled down the wicket towards me, stopped up close and personal. Extending a right arm, he patted me on my left shoulder: "Aye, yoooung man, thar's proper rcspect. Thankee."

Wicket-keeper Meads, slip Keeton and my partner Jim Bailey were laughing. I was chuckling, too! Twenty minutes later I was bowled for 23 by Bill Sime.

Thirty years later, while studying for a Masters Degree in Social Work at the University of Sussex, Alan wrote a psychology essay on 'Decisions and Consequences', in which he relived his encounter with Charlie Harris.

DECISION: Yes, I had made the decision to bat-pad that slow high-flighted ball out of respect for the status and reputation of a veteran opponent. Yes, I was, then, a greenhorn in the norms and mores of professional cricket.

CONSEQUENCES: Did I learn from the experience? Yes! Did I apply the lesson learned? Yes, but not consistently. In my ten seasons with Hampshire I was not consistent as a run-making county cricketer – as against being a consistent fielder at cover point.

What if I had reversed that decision and attacked the 'tempter' that Charlie Harris offered, deliberately, to test me? I had not been unnerved by his comment nor lost concentration and would have hit a six unless I had not hit the ball cleanly and had been caught at slip or mid-off. 'Tis all conjecture, but I think that the very experienced Charlie Harris 'read me' as a confident, fit, athletic young man who had had little experience of the 'mind games' and art of 'gamesmanship' practised in those days by some, not all, experienced first-class cricketers – club players, too. I believe his elementary 'mind game' was a test to see whether I would try to hit his 'tempter' for six, and probably be caught, or would play an orthodox forward defensive stroke and thus prove to himself his power to control the behaviour of a young, inexperienced, professional batsman.

I played the latter. I still dream the former.

*

In the second innings, needing to score quick runs ahead of a declaration, Alan was caught at slip for 9. Nottinghamshire were set to score 263 in 3¾ hours and looked on course for victory at 212 for four. Then off-spinner Charlie Knott was brought back into the attack, a wicket fell, and in strode Frank Woodhead who, batting at number eleven in the first innings, had hit a lusty 40 in 19 minutes. A few blows from him, and the game would be all but won. Off-spinner Jim Bailey was bowling from the Stadium end, and Alan was despatched to long-on in front of a huddle of friendly spectators. It was a scene that Alan enjoyed recreating for this book.

"Aye, Blondee, them up tharr Midlums be 'ardy folk, ah reckuns," opined one of a dozen pensioners sitting on planks in the shade of the Stadium fence.

"Arrh, an' Blondee 'ere be arr noo yungun … look'n good feldarr," replied his mate from farmlands deep in Hampshire's Downs.

"Ayee, yungun, weem gotta get 'im out or 'e'll win it ferum in no time!"

"Yer new, aintchyer ? Wherr d'yer cum frum? ... Ohaaar, Lurnun ... Posh place arrbet ... Lurd's ... Yernoa Compton?"

Jim Bailey bowled, and Woodhead hoicked a six over mid-wicket into the gardens of Hamtum House Hotel. As I moved back three yards to stand on the boundary line, a voice from the Huddle ten feet away called out: "Ope yer gerd a' catchin', mate, cos arr reccun ones acomin diswaays."

Bailey bowled again. Woodhead slogged again but straighter and higher – very high – and the ball was coming my way. There was time for opinions to be vocalised among rural voices in The Huddle.

"Lukyrr, mate ... Up darr ... Ees 'igh be darr ... Comin' arr way ... Corrr."

Yes, Woodhead had hit a steepler, but I was not sure whether it would descend to my right or left ... or over my head.

"Yungun's goin' ferr-it ... arr ... naah ... too 'igh ... 'ee wun catch daar ..."

"Naah ... barrr'ees unnerr ... over 'is 'ed ... naah ..."

No ... no ... about five yards in front of me ... slow dance forward and slightly left ... a bit more left ... hands skyward ... cupped together ten inches in front of my eyes ... total focus on that rapidly descending ball ... into cupped-hands-fingers closed and ball caressed to my chest ... GOT IT!

"YERR, 'EES GORIT ... 'EES GORN AN' BLEEDIN' CORIT!"

The Huddle were standing, clapping and calling out: "*Well daarn, yungun ... Well caaart!*"

I turned, ball still in cupped hands clasped to my chest, bowed to the Huddle, then become aware of a crescendo of applause going around the ground as I walked towards centre stage and tossed the ball to Jim Bailey.

"Well caught, Punchy ... it was up there a long time ... well judged," quipped smiling team-mates. A few handshakes, praise from the Skipper and one gentle pat on a shoulder from Gerry Hill.

No communal 'love-in' back in far-off '49! Perhaps there should have been for Charlie Knott when he took four of the last five wickets for ten runs! But again 'not in those days' – far, far too embarrassing – just not part of the old social culture when cricketers were dressed in subtle shades of white, according to pocket or preference.

Everyone in the Hutch, in the Pavilion, in the Members' Bar was in high spirits, as were a couple of hundred fans milling around in front of the Pavilion – shaking hands, thumping each other on the back – laughing – calling out to each other – excited – happy that our veteran spinners had bowled out 'them 'ardy ol' pros' and won the first home match of the season. Jim Bailey bowled 45 overs, four wickets; Gerry Hill 42 overs, four wickets, and Charlie Knott took 12 wickets in 58 overs. They were hardy, too!

Congratulations and pints galore in The Hutch – young Alan a half, then another half in the Members' Bar, chatting with team mates and the old pros of Nottinghamshire, including Charlie Harris.

It was six-day-a-week cricket now, and at 7.15 the next morning Alan was at the County Ground, boarding a bumpy Bedford coach (standing in for the cosy Albion) for the journey to Taunton.

My team mates were in various states of wakefulness following their exertions in the field yesterday. A few of our veterans may have enjoyed a pint too many, reminiscing with those other old pros.

In an unobtrusive, avuncular manner Neil McCorkell and Gerry Hill continued to shepherd this socially confident freshman through his virgin weeks of county cricket – a mobile apprenticeship in sport and the University of Life. I was lapping up experiences of new people and places, new sights and sounds – and it was love at first sight as I trod the turf of Taunton's cricket ground, set in the centre of a thriving West Country town, squeezed between the 14th century St James Church and the River Tone.

Having lost the toss, Desmond Eagar led us through the crowded members' pavilion. Warm-hearted applause from the members and a thousand or so spectators heralded Somerset's opening pair: the legendary, hard-hitting Harold Gimblett accompanied by Eric Hill, a young professional who later became a well-known journalist in the West Country.

Amateur Vic Ransom, our cheerful butcher from Guildford, had been called up to strengthen our seam bowling attack, and our jovial soccer and cricket international Johnny Arnold was fit enough to play his first match of the season. Johnny and I were both specialist fielders at cover point and, as expected, Skipper directed 'Junior' to mid-off.

The sun was shining, the wicket hard, the conversational buzz from expectant spectators muted as Gimblett faced Shack's first ball – on the spot and played defensively. The second ball was also on the spot, but this time it was met by the thud of willow on leather. Then in a flash of time the ball was in the air and stinging my hands, which were splayed by the power of the drive. I was stunned motionless, muttering to myself, "I don't drop catches, I don't drop catches – but I have."

"RAYMENT!!" bellowed the skipper from short leg. "Get after it!"

I turned, sprinted but failed to save the boundary, and I walked slowly back to mid-off, mortified. I had dropped Harold Gimblett – Gimblett on nought!! My guilt was not assuaged when I caught Hill for 13 and Woodhouse for 10 because Harold Gimblett thundered on to score 115 in a total of 242.

Johnny Arnold and Neville Rogers took Hampshire to 38 for no wicket at close of play. With no cricket the next day, the team set off for some welcome Saturday night relaxation.

This was the first season in which the Hampshire team wore 'away-day bow ties', an idea introduced by Jim Bailey and Charlie Knott. They were navy-blue clip-ons, which had a small yellow rose embroidered into each of the four corners of the front bow. Members of the team were obliged to wear them on the first day of an away match or be fined five shillings, the money paid into a 'beer fund' for a celebration later in the season.

The bow ties caused comments both ribald and humorous from the Somerset players as we shared a drink at the bar before walking through the narrow streets of Taunton to the County Hotel, a pleasant Georgian building in need of interior refurbishment.

A dance in the hotel ballroom was sold out, but during dinner Neville Rogers and twelfth man Tom Dean came up with a plan to overcome this.

With Big Tom in the lead six of us, resplendent in navy-blue blazers and unconventional bow ties, walked boldly past the startled ticket staff, proclaiming one by one: "Band ... Interval band ... Er, band ... Thank you ... Band!"

Wow! Harry Gold and His Pieces Of Eight were on stage. Leading the premier British Dixieland band of the era, Harry Gold played several instruments but had a particular penchant for playing the huge contrabass saxophone. Harry's ensemble had the packed audience jumpin' and jivin', a scene I revelled in but which made Gerry Hill feel uncomfortable. As our four team-mates headed for the bar, I shouted in Gerry's ear – a mere whisper considering the din – "Come with me up the steps to the wings; I want to watch the musicians."

Gerry felt safer away from the energetic dancers but covered his ears because we were closer to the powerful speakers. Halfway through 'Tiger Rag' the amplification cut out. The singer pulled his mike off the stand and tap-tapped it – no response. The musicians played on; the buzz in the dance crowd faded.

Gerry gave me a puzzled look. I looked down at his feet, grabbed his arm and hastened down the steps to lose ourselves in the crowd. "What's happening?" Gerry asked, perplexed.

"You trod on a wire lead. They've probably got some heavy chaps in their crew. Best we disappear before they find out!"

On Sunday morning he and Cliff Walker went for a walk through the streets and along the river before returning to the hotel for a lunch that would mark another moment of importance in his journey towards acceptance in the side.

Picture in your mind a drab, poorly-lit hotel dining room cluttered with dark Victorian furniture and large gilt-framed oil paintings of no consequence and little value. A group of sportsmen dressed in various styles of navy blue blazers and sports jackets – ties, of course – took their places at a long Tudor-style table, classically appointed with white damask cloths, heavy silver-plated cutlery, side plates, baskets filled with bread rolls, condiment sets, water jugs and glasses. A polite murmur and nodding of heads in our direction from other diners as we, a well-mannered yet boisterous and hungry – really hungry – group of cricketers, settled into our seats, perused menus and flapped open coned, linen serviettes. Three elderly bald-headed, stooped-shouldered male waiters dressed in crumpled ill-fitting black waistcoated suits – who in my imagination had emerged from the guilt-framed oil paintings – took our orders and, almost ethereally, faded into a dimly lit corner and disappeared.

We waited ... lots of chat and laughter, of course ... and then waited as our splendid raconteur Jim Bailey rolled through a tall tale ... and waited. The three wobbly waiters processed slowly from the kitchen door to our table, each carrying a large tray laid with three soup bowls, followed by a sprightly young kitchen lad who managed to juggle four soups on an even larger tray to complete the serving to twelve players and the scorer, Len Sprankling.

I broke my bread roll and nearly broke into a loud expletive but, turning to my neighbour Shack, quietly mimicked, "Eee lud, wer's t'bleedin' soup?" In the middle of my bowl there was a white island surrounded by a narrow moat of brown liquid.

Hungry cricketers? Well, I was the youngest and the hungriest, and I was cross – but in control. I got up from my seat and approached Desmond Eagar at the head of the table. The chatter stopped ... heads turned in our direction as I whispered: "Skipper, there is a white island in the middle of my soup, and I wish to complain to the chef in the kitchen."

Desmond thought for a brief moment, then replied: "There's not much soup in my bowl, either, Alan, nor the others. Hmm, well, Alan, as long as you are very polite you may talk to the chef in the kitchen."

Team-mates within hearing range – many of them ex-servicemen – piped up: "Go on, young Al, see if you can get us better rations ... You've got a nerve, nipper, but good luck anyway."

Except for cockroach-infested kitchens at RAF Padgate I had had no experience of commercial kitchens – though I remembered comic scenes from 1930s films and therefore approached the two-way swing doors with caution. Inside I encountered steam but little noise, four staff, no film-style commotion, the head chef immediately recognisable not only by his tall white hat and full apron but by his size, his confident demeanour and bushy ginger moustache.

Surprised to see a young blond lad in smart blazer, grey flannels and tie, the burly chef walked past the ovens and preparation tables, wiping his hands on a chequered cloth, then held out his right hand to shake mine: "Well, young man, you look like one of the cricketers staying here. What can I do for you?"

"Mr Chef, your brown soup is probably delicious, but there is so little on my plate that it will be hard to judge. Is it possible to serve the hungry members of our team with an extra helping of your undoubtedly excellent soup?"

Pausing, grinning broadly and looking me in the eye, he announced: "Undoubtedly, young man, undoubtedly *(chuckle)*. It will be my honour to serve the hungry Hampshires ... personally. You return to your table." *(still chuckling)*

The buzz of questions from my team mates caused murmurs among the other diners – and questioning looks – murmurs that became audible chatter when Mr Burly Chef entered the dining room resplendent in full whites and tall hat, brandishing a ladle, accompanied by the kitchen boy gingerly pushing a serving trolley transporting a large steaming urn across the worn carpet.

"Gentlemen, welcome to our County Hotel. I understand from that young man *(ladle flourished towards yours truly)* that you are hungry. Well, with my compliments, fill yourselves with soup from this urn but be sure to leave room for the excellent roast beef and Yorkshires that follow. Enjoy your match tomorrow."

Mr Burly Chef acknowledged our plaudits and hastened to his duties in the kitchen, leaving his young assistant to ladle large quantities of the steaming liquid into our bowls. The Skipper paid me a cheerful compliment, and the general banter became fruity – about soup. However, I soon realised that I had unconsciously cast myself in the role of diplomatic negotiator with hotel managers and staff when on tour, unless the issues were of a more serious or monetary nature. Such matters were dealt with by the Skipper or businessman Charlie Knott.

Alan's next memory of that trip to Taunton was of experiencing a sensation that was strange to him then but which he came to recognise later in his life.

On the bright, fresh and cloudless Monday morning I was enjoying the team's net practice when something rose up from deep within me – something 'other' – something I did not understand at the time. I had bowled several medium-paced deliveries to Neil McCorkell and, when retrieving a ball some distance from the nets, stooped to pick up the ball, stopped, looked around and surveyed the ground.

My mind 'filmed' the shapes and colours of the 'now', then seemed to refocus to scenes of, and feel of, the past: famous players of yesteryear emerging from a small old-style pavilion being applauded by people dressed in Edwardian attire sitting on hard seats in wooden stands – a big old roller with horse shafts, heavy wooden sight screens and primitive public toilets balanced by the architectural magnificence of the historic church towers: St James guarding a boundary edge and St Mary Magdalene in the middle distance beyond third man.

A déjà-vu experience?

Hampshire were well beaten, bowled out for totals of 150 and 144, with Alan making 16 and 10. But his main memory of the last two days was of a moment in the Somerset second innings when Gimblett was once more attacking the bowling.

As I was crossing the wicket from mid-off to mid-off at the end of an over, Desmond Eagar walked towards me and said, "Try an over at this end, Alan."

I froze, brain numbed. Me bowl? Me? Speechless! My medium quick in-swingers, successful in my club and RAF days, had been given the thumbs-down by Arthur Holt and the senior professionals. My throat emitted a nervous cough as I attempted to respond to the captain's polite command: "Umm, errr, thank you, skipper. I think one slip, otherwise save the four."

The shock that had frozen my mind gave way to an awareness of the reality, of the wholly unexpected privilege to make my Hampshire debut as a bowler. I paced out my fourteen-pace run, scratched a mark in the damp turf with my boot studs and turned to face my opponent at the batting crease. There, tapping his bat in the block hole, was Harold Gimblett. His rolled-up shirt sleeves revealed forearms as muscular as Popeye's, and his warm-hearted demeanour belied a fiery competitive spirit within. The scoreboard stated that his score was 94. Respect shot up to nerve-tingling awe!

I sensed the surprised interest of my team-mates and noted that wicket-keeper Neil McCorkell was up to the stumps. As I turned to commence my run-up I muttered to myself, "Pitch it up, pitch it up."

I released the spongy ball – ooops – a medium-paced long-hop. Before I had finished my follow-through, the sad ball was disappearing out of the ground to splash down in the River Tone.

Applause for the six and Harold Gimblett's second hundred in the match. My two overs cost 25 runs.

*

In 2008, on a Dorset Cricket Society outing to Taunton, Alan told the tale of Harold Gimblett's six. Overhearing him, a workman presented him with a ball: "I've just fished this out of the river. Perhaps it's the one you bowled."

Alan's memories of his remaining first-team games that summer were few. In a rain-ruined match at Bristol, when they threw their bats in a last-ditch attempt to gain the points for first-innings lead, he went in at number nine and was caught for a duck. Then back at Southampton, in the traditional Whit Bank Holiday fixture against Kent, he played in the last of the six matches he had been promised. He batted at number nine, below Derek Shackleton, scoring 3 and 9 not out.

He was dropped for the next match but returned for the trip to Northampton, his last appearance in the championship that summer.

> In our second innings Shack and I held up their victory in an eighth-wicket partnership of 68, which also held up the taxis to the railway station. No time for a shower or social pleasantries. Steam train to Euston, taxis to Waterloo, home late.
>
> Next morning at Northlands Road a beaming Arthur Holt took me aside and told me that I was to report to The Hutch.
>
> "Why, Arthur?"
>
> "Skipper wants you as twelfth man for the tourist match. It's your fielding. There'll be a big crowd. If anyone is injured, you can show off in the outfield."

The New Zealanders were the tourists. Despite playing Test matches intermittently for almost twenty years, they were yet to enjoy a victory and would not do so for another seven years. Nevertheless they had some fine players, notably two left-handed batsmen Martin Donnelly and Bert Sutcliffe. Ably led by Walter Hadlee, father of Sir Richard, they were more than a match for the county sides they played, and in a warm summer they attracted good crowds wherever they went. The Hampshire game was no exception.

> An on-field appearance for a twelfth man was rare, the role mainly that of team butler: a lot of tray carrying from the dreary kitchen under the Members' Stand, up steps, down steps, past unsighted, unwary members, up stairs into the Hutch with tea, sandwiches and cakes for fourteen ... at close of play a variety of alcoholic beverages and one milk ... a pint of milk ... for whom? Before play some pads or boots to whiten, plasters to find and fags to buy from the bar. Oh and bowl in the nets to any player any time, be diplomatic host to VIPs when Hampshire were in the field and guardsman to stop autograph hunters and other cheeky intruders reaching the top of the stairs to the Hutch.
>
> 'No stewards?' I hear you say – I'm chuckling! In 1949?
>
> During play the butler was occasionally required to trot to the wicket with dry batting gloves, a sweater, a roll of white tape to bandage a bat and, on really scorching days, drinks for players and umpires. On one such trot to the middle I was carrying an aluminium 'box' under a sweater and returned with a concave model turned inside out by a quick bowler. Ouch!
>
> Ah! But I've missed out a most important role – to look after the visitor's twelfth man! The New Zealanders' twelfth man would not have been to Southampton, would need to be 'genned up' about everything and introduced to the assistant secretary, the groundsman, the umpires' room, the telephone box - and the catering manager, if we had one.

It was a wonderful game of cricket, one that stayed in Alan's memory. The New Zealanders, with a stylish cerntury from Martin Donnelly, built a first-innings lead of 301, but Hampshire seemed to have saved the game, thanks in part to a century from the veteran Johnny Arnold.

> As I write, a feeling of 'happy-sadness' wells up from the depths, and I *sense* Johnny Arnold ... *see* him batting ... beautifully ... bat raised

high, acknowledging waves of warm-hearted applause ... a century ... unknown then, it was his last in front of a home crowd.

Neil McCorkell, Johnny's team-mate since 1932, scored 67, Desmond Eagar 82, and Hampshire were all out for 409, leaving the New Zealanders the seemingly impossible target of scoring 109 in 39 minutes to win the match.

Two world-class left-handers opened the batting; the artist Donnelly and the muscleman Sutcliffe, By grace and power they plundered 49 in the first four overs, Sutcliffe hit 46 in 13 minutes, and the New Zealanders won the match with five minutes to spare.

Imagine the excitement, the applause – and the forever memory in the minds of all cricket lovers who were *there-then;* who saw, felt, heard and were caught up in the joyful tension of that unforgettable climax of a cricket match played *in the spirit of the game!*

Eleven overs and five balls were delivered in 34 minutes by seam bowlers; the Hampshire fielders not only retrieved balls from under the plank stands beyond the boundary ropes but ran to their new positions between overs. The incoming batsmen ran to the wicket, and the umpires hastened from square-leg to the stumps.

At 'stumps' Desmond Eagar hurried across to shake Walter Hadlee's hand – most vigorously. And though I was late getting the tray of drinks up the stairs into the Hutch, because excited arm-waving members were almost impassable, I too was caught up in the euphoria of the moment – a moment fading in detail but still powerfully felt somewhere deep inside me.

*

Alan's only further first-class match that summer was against the Combined Services at Portsmouth. In all, in eight first-class games, he scored a disappointing 133 runs at an average of 12.09, His highest score was the 35 he hit at Northampton, batting with Derek Shackleton when the match was all but lost and his team-mates were anxious to climb into the taxis.

Yet Alan was not disheartened. He had another year of his contract to run, and he had far too optimistic a nature to look at the empty half of the glass.

> I had achieved my childhood dream to play county cricket; my cup of experience and learning filled to the brim; my examination marks high in fielding, very low in runs acquired. No matter, I was thankful for the experience and determined to improve my defensive batting,

become more selective in using my quiverful of attacking shots and learn more about bowlers' techniques and ways of 'thinking you out'.

Daily life in my first summer as a professional cricketer was, in so many aspects, a dream far beyond my dreams of yesteryear, a life ensconced in the cocoon of a national sport that shielded us from involvement in, and exposure to, many negative realities of daily life, in our country and around the world.

As an avid reader of the daily newspapers during and after the war and a habitual listener to BBC radio news – a good habit instilled by my dear Father to whom 'the six pips' heralded *SILENCE* – I maintained an awareness of national and international affairs.

Britain's Labour government under Prime Minister Clement Attlee continued their programmes to establish a Welfare State but were hampered, as would have been any government in power at that time, by the slow economic recovery after the war. Pressures on our gold reserves, mainly due to our deficits with the USA and Canada, led to a 30 percent devaluation of the pound in September which increased shortages in the supply of essential materials.

To cope with our tight budget Betty and I purchased a long metal money box which had eight sections, each with a coin slot on the lid. We apportioned our weekly cash (£2–5s 1d) into sections labelled food/clothes/baby/bus fares/electricity/savings. Betty and I had savings of about forty pounds in a Post Office account. We were concerned about the forthcoming increase in our budget when, and after, the baby arrived but convinced ourselves that income from the winter job, promised by the county club, would be more than adequate to cover those costs.

Fortunately we were both strong-minded, confident and supportive of each other: we did not expect financial support from senior members in our family because, although caring and in regular communication with us, none were 'well off'.

*

Hampshire, with only six wins in 26 championship matches, finished 16th out of 17, down seven places from the previous year, but nobody at the club was downcast. As the magazine *The Cricketer* put it in its end-of-season summary, 'Rebuilding a side is a long and painful business but the cry today is for youth and whatever the results show at the end of next season the policy of giving youth a chance must bear fruit in the next few years.'

Derek Shackleton had an outstanding year, scoring 914 runs and taking 100 wickets, and the 2nd XI, playing for the first time in the Minor Counties Championship, finished in third place. Leading the run-scoring in the team were a trio of young hopefuls: Jimmy Gray, David Guard and Alan.

> From mid-June to early September I played a lot of cricket for Hampshire 2nd XI and Club & Ground teams with and against an array of characters on a variety of grounds, from town turf to village green, learning something of the geography, the social atmosphere, the people and places of my newly adopted county. It was all so new, so interesting and exciting.

Special in Alan's 2nd XI season were a century against Wiltshire and two matches against Middlesex 2nd XI, when he met up with former team-mates. The home fixture against Middlesex was at the Victoria Recreation Ground in Newport on the Isle of Wight, an island which Alan knew well from childhood holidays and which was always dear to him.

> A quirky memory: David Guard, the amateur who was ten days older than me, arrived by taxi, having flown from the mainland to Bembridge airport in a small private aeroplane – a *happening* that gave rise to *mutterings* among the *lowly* paid professionals.

The away match was at Finchley's Arden Field, a few yards from where Alan was born and where he fell in love with the game. It was the last 2nd XI fixture of the summer and, had they taken two more Middlesex wickets and thus won and not drawn the game, they would have qualified for the play-off match for the championship.

The summer of 1949 was the sunniest since 1911, the driest of the whole 20th century, and Alan was loving his new life away from the metropolis.

> Occasionally that summer, and many times during the next four years, we travelled by bus or train to venues in the New Forest and bordering coastal villages, to Winchester, Romsey and other places of historic interest. Our friend Bob scrounged enough petrol coupons that summer to take us to beaches at Barton on Sea and Mudeford; on one occasion he drove my parents and brother Derek from London in his Austin 10 to meet us at the County Ground where I was playing in a Club & Ground match.
>
> Although I had now tasted three-day county cricket, observed first-hand the higher levels of skills and the feel of a wider public

audience, I thoroughly enjoyed meeting and playing with and against the club cricketers of Hampshire throughout the rest of the season. So many delightful venues, interesting characters, skilled players – and stalwart men and women members who maintained pavilions and grounds, organised playing and social facilities and raised money to keep the clubs solvent.

Desmond Eagar was passionate about cricket and about Hampshire cricket in particular, not only the county championship but all levels of the game in all places throughout the county. Wholeheartedly supported by Arthur Holt and the President Harry Altham, he promoted the game with missionary zeal around the county, speaking in schools and clubs, in village community halls and at city lunch meetings.

Desmond also developed and maintained close associations with the editors of local newspapers and with cricket writers covering the national press. His friendship with John Arlott was classically fruitful in raising the profile of Hampshire cricket. From his appointment as Captain and Secretary in 1946, Desmond Eagar's enthusiastic promotion of the game of cricket and its culture had, by 1949, already produced an upsurge of goodwill towards the county's cricket club.

This was never more apparent than in the fortnight after Hampshire ended their first-class season. While the cricketers of many counties departed to winter jobs, the Hampshire players embarked on a round of friendly matches, culminating in a game at Bournemouth against the Duke of Edinburgh's XI.

First came a trip to the Isle of Wight where the Hampshire side played at Ventnor, Newport and St Helens. The last of these fixtures, against a Villages XI, was played on a picturesque green, long and narrow, set between two roads lined with housing and shops. Some of the Hampshire team laid small bets on hitting the roofs of the houses, and Alan duly did so, breaking a tile, just as he had done in May when he hit Charlie Harris for six.

The following week they were in the far north of the county, on the historic Green at Hartley Wintney, where the village laid on a great day.

'Dressed up' aptly sums up my first and overall impression of Hartley Wintney in festival mode. There was brightly coloured bunting everywhere: in the village centre, on the edge of the Common, by the Parish Church, along Cricket Lane and all around the Green. A Festival, a Carnival, a Celebration: no word can match the joyful spirit of community that touched us all that day, a spirit that may have been associated with a remnant of post-war euphoria, though more probably linked with the long history of cricket in the village and its local enthusiasm for the game.

A boys' band played before the match and during the intervals, beating the retreat at close of play. There was a fully licensed marquee on the ground and in the evening a 'Grand Non-Stop Dance' at the village's Victoria Hall. Before the dance Alan remembers the team being entertained at his house, The Grange, by Adrian Stoop, the former Harlequins and England rugby player (after whom the Harlequins' ground, The Stoop, is named). A decorated war hero, he was the President of the Hartley Wintney Cricket Club.

The match was won in style by the county team, with a century from Sam Pothecary, the pre-war Hampshire cricketer, now a first-class umpire. Alan's last innings of the summer yielded 14 runs.

Five days later Alan was among the 10,000 and more at Dean Park, Bournemouth, who gathered for an enthralling match between Hampshire and the Duke of Edinburgh's XI. Prince Philip, flying down from Balmoral, skippered a side that included Denis Compton, Gubby Allen, Freddie Brown and Walter Robins, and in the dying moments of the day, chasing 255, they won by one wicket, the winning run coming from a lofted mishit that narrowly evaded a fielder.

The young royal bowled nine tidy overs (one for 25) and scored a brisk 13 runs including two stylish drives for four before – in the words of one report – 'paying the price for impetuosity'. The umpire Frank Chester was impressed: "The Duke surprised me by his ability and keenness. With regular play I'm sure he would make a good 'un."

3

A lifelong friendship
Tim Biles

When Alan was writing the chapters of this book during 2020, he was one of the last survivors of county cricket in the 1940s. He played seven championship matches in 1949, and by 2020 there was no other survivor from any of them. Furthermore, after the death of Malcolm Heath in December 2019, Alan's only living team-mate from his ten years in the Hampshire side was Derek Tulk, a stalwart of the Old Tauntonians club who played one match for the county in each of 1956 and 1957. Alan had outlived almost all his contemporaries.

His one surviving friend from those days was the Reverend Canon Timothy Biles, whom he met almost as soon as he arrived at the County Ground in the spring of 1949. For this book Alan left a short chapter on Tim, which he constructed from conversations with him.

Alan and Tim Biles

In 1946 Tim was eleven years old, living with his family in Westrow Gardens, a cul-de-sac off Northlands Road. A gap in the back-garden hedge allowed Tim to get into the area where the team practised in the nets, and this led to the start of a close relationship with the players. This is how Alan wrote up what Tim told him:

> I could watch the players practise at close quarters. Later I dared to stand behind the bowlers to gather balls hit out of the nets and roll them back to the bowlers. No one took any notice of me until one day a powerful low drive came straight for my face. Instinctively I put my hands in front of my face – and caught the ball! All hell broke loose among the bowlers closest to me: "That could have killed him! ... Who is that kid? ... What's he doing here?"
>
> Then came an authoritative voice, booming from the far side of the nursery ground: "Well caught, son, you'll play for Hampshire" and, to the professionals, "Encourage the boy, encourage the boy!" *The Voice* was that of Desmond Eagar. From that moment on, I was accepted and befriended by the professionals, almost like a mascot – never to play but soon to become the second-eleven scorer.

A group of boys at Easter coaching at Southampton in 1949
Far left is Tim Biles

In this role of occasional 2nd XI scorer he came to the attention of the club's official scorer Len Sprankling, and in 1948 this led to his selling scorecards at the ground when the Australians visited in June.

> After I had sold my allocation of scorecards and pocketed the commission of a halfpenny per card, I was invited to join Mr Sprankling in the scorebox to watch the game. I sat on a stool just behind him and the Australian scorer, Mr Ferguson. What a privilege! I have never forgotten how impressed I was that Mr Ferguson not only maintained his own complex scoresheet alongside the standard scorebook of the time but also sketched the ground as seen from the scorebox. If he did that everywhere he went, he must have created a marvellous and unique record of the world's cricket grounds in the post-war era. Also, in addition to scribing the two scorebooks and sketching the ground, Mr Ferguson created something I had never seen before: a 'wagon-wheel' chart depicting where each batsman scored their runs. I was amazed!
>
> I must have behaved myself because Mr Ferguson gave me a pile of papers which turned out to be the official autograph sheets of the entire Australian touring team, headed by Don Bradman. I gave some to school friends – showing off, I suppose – but I kept one for myself and sold it at auction in 2018 for £1,000.

Bill Ferguson was back in 1950, scoring for the West Indian tourists, and by this time Tim, now a 15-year-old, was creating wagon wheels himself, each match selecting a favourite player.

> They must have been rather rough because I did not possess a protractor, as Fergie had, and the chart got messy when the lines kept crossing as they emerged from each wicket. When the West Indies came to Southampton Frank Worrell was not playing so I decided to make a wagon wheel for Everton Weekes.
>
> It was my lucky choice because he went on to score 246 not out. But oh, my chart! I had never imagined a wagon wheel beyond a hundred and a few; this one looked a terrible mess! I couldn't believe my luck when the West Indies assistant manager offered me ten shillings for it. My first real earnings!

Alan had arrived on the staff the previous summer, 1949, and he remembered the first time he spoke with Tim.

We shared a friendly chat on the steps of the Members' Pavilion following afternoon net practice. He was keen to know about the players who had been my team-mates in the Middlesex 2nd XI and the Royal Air Force. A few days later, after I had scored a fifty in the Over-30s versus Under-30s match, I was surprised and delighted when he presented me with a wagon-wheel chart of my innings.

When not at school, Tim was ever present as scorer for Club & Ground and 2nd XI matches – and retrieving balls at net practice – throughout the season. Intelligent and cheerful, friendly and well-mannered, he was respected by the 2nd XI skipper Basil Bowyer and befriended by the younger professionals and by Arthur Holt, who was a particular friend to Tim in his schoolboy years and on into his professional life.

In 1958, as a young adult, Tim became a 'ten-pound pom', emigrating to Australia where he hoped to watch the forthcoming Ashes series. His early attempts to find work in Adelaide were fruitless till he saw a blackboard in the street: 'Wanted: Office Clerk, Apply Within'. It was a stockbroker's firm, and the receptionist ushered him through to see the boss, who turned out to be Don Bradman.

"What do you know about stockbroking?" the Don asked, and Tim, thinking a stockbroker was someone who rounded up cattle, said, "I can't ride a horse, but I'm willing to learn." This greatly tickled Bradman, who promptly took him on. He was a hopeless clerk, but the Don and his family took a great liking to him, and at the end of his stay they gave him the great man's Test blazer and cap.

Tim was a very special man in Alan's life:

> He became a close friend of our family, is godfather to one of the children and now, in 2020, the dear friend that I have known for the longest time.
>
> Retired and living in Dorset with his wife Joan, he is the published author of eleven books, full of wisdom and humour. He has lived an extraordinary life, full of colour and variety. He has given so much to so many people and is as enthusiastic and emotional about the roller-coaster fortunes of Hampshire cricket as he was when we first met 71 years ago. I am blessed to be his friend.

4

Books, cows and nappies
Winter 1949/50

The county club had failed abjectly in its promise to find Alan accommodation in the spring, and it fared no better when it came to their promise to find him winter employment. By late August he had heard nothing and, with Betty now seven months pregnant, he was growing worried. In a break between matches he arranged an appointment to see Desmond Eagar in his office.

Eagar was profusely apologetic, assuring Alan that he would follow this up immediately with the committee. Then he startled Alan by saying that, if no job had come up by the end of September, he personally would pay him three pounds a week to index and catalogue the books in the club's cricket library. Further, in case Alan was offered a job that entailed driving, he would pay for some driving lessons and a test. "Your co-ordination is good," he said cheerfully. "You should pass first time."

> Surprised? No, overwhelmed! As I expressed my thanks to the Skipper, adding that I looked forward to cataloguing the library books, I felt the need to excuse myself before my emotions overflowed. 'So generous,' I kept muttering to myself as I raced home on my bike to share the wonderful news with Betty, who responded with her own good news.
>
> "Darling, I have found a place to live where the landlady will accept us with the baby! We can move in after the first Monday in September."

With the help of their friend Bob, who drove his Austin 10 down from London, they moved their belongings – no furniture – into two large rooms at 58 Radway Road, off Hill Lane, a detached house backing onto the playing fields of the Girls' High School. The owner, Mrs Burke, had been a nurse when she was young. A baby was no problem for her.

Alan followed up various job adverts in the *Daily Echo*, but at the end of September he was no further forward so he reported to Desmond Eagar and began the task of sorting out the books in the library, pasting a club plate inside the cover of each book. It was an imaginative venture, one about which Eagar wrote in the 1951 members' handbook:

> Hampshire is fortunate in possessing a large and varied Cricket Library. This came to the Club as a gift from the Hampshire players and was one of the direct benefits from a 'Players' Aid To County Fund'. For two years after the war the Players themselves raised over £1,000 for their Club. This was something unique in the annals of professional sport.
>
> A number of Members and Cricket Lovers have given books as gifts for the Library, and their generosity is much appreciated. All books, pictures and other items of Cricketana are always a most welcome addition to the assets or the Club. It is of interest that the well known author and broadcaster Mr John Arlott always presents a copy of his latest book to us.
>
> The very lovely Club Book plate is inserted in each book. There is also a Catalogue and Card Index available for the use of Members. The first book was taken out of the Library on the 9th of February 1948. Since then over 500 books have been borrowed, and returned safely.

Discovering this article seventy years later, Alan felt a 'humble pride' that he had created the first catalogue and card index system for the books.

> And I was reminded, of course, of Desmond Eagar's caring generosity in paying me £3 a week from his private income. Equally the fees for driving lessons and the test, which I passed driving a 1938 Morris 8hp in the midst of a heavy thunderstorm and torrential rain.
>
> No flashing indicators in those days. Every signal had to be conducted by extending the right arm outside the car – the window wound down and up by the right hand. Huge raindrops battering the roof sounded like a continuous drum-roll and drenched my right arm and shoulder through my rubberised trench-coat.
>
> At the infamous Seven Dials roundabout I had to wait in a queue of traffic, could not hear the engine and consequently thought I had stalled and failed my test. Thankfully Mr Examiner could not hear the engine, told me to declutch and – hey presto – Morris 8 eased its way beyond Seven Dials back to the depot. Mr Examiner congratulated me on my calmness during the storm and handed me a form on which he had written *Pass*.

*Alan back at the wheel of a Morris 8
while attending a day recreating the 1940s at Alresford*

The big event of the year – much more important than my Hampshire debut or any other cricket match – was the birth of our first child in Southampton General Hospital on Saturday 15 October.

Knowing that Betty and I had spent the last of our savings on all the other preparations for the arrival of our first son or daughter, my parents and cousins in London had kindly funded a new Silver Cross pram and a cot. We were counting our pennies; I was counting on selling something so that I could buy Betty some flowers on my first visit after the birth.

Neither of us had any qualms or anxieties leading up to *the event*. We presumed, perhaps naively, that Betty would experience a straightforward *normal* birth and that the baby would be *normal* too.

Our innocent assumptions were fulfilled. Betty, a fit young woman with a strong constitution, gave birth to a son weighing 7lb 4oz – no complications. However, although I remember that Betty and the baby remained in hospital for about a week, I needed to check the true facts and phoned her today (8 March 2019). She laughed when I asked, "Were you really in hospital for seven days?"

"No, Alan, ten days," she replied, "and I was not allowed out of bed for nine days!"

"NINE DAYS IN BED," I exclaimed loudly. "You're not kidding me, are you? Not even to go to the toilet?"

"Not even. It was bedpans only."

During the afternoon of Saturday 15 October this proud 21-year-old husband and father walked into the hospital ward carrying a big bunch of red and yellow roses. I felt excited yet serene when holding our baby for the first time ... and beyond happy when hugging Betty cradling our new-born son.

We were very conscious of our responsibilities as young parents; the wartime experiences of our generation had forged responsible adulthood before we were sixteen and, for the men-boys, compulsory service in the armed forces from the age of eighteen had, for most of us, tempered the values of duty, service and responsibility.

How did I pay for those red and yellow roses? I sold my portable wind-up gramophone, my most treasured childhood possession which had been a Christmas present from my godmother in 1932. A second-hand dealer in Shirley gave me thirty shillings, and I spent three shilling on the roses.

Looking back to those roses and the sale of that gramophone, I realise that it was in its way a rite of passage.

*

The Christian 'rite of passage', the Baptism of our son took place at St Mark's Church, Southampton, soon after Christmas. Betty and I had agreed on the names Denis Gerald Alan – Denis in respect of Denis Compton, Gerald after Gerry Hill who had been such a friendly mentor before and during my matches in the first eleven, and Alan as a traditional link between father and eldest son.

From the moment that Betty and Denis returned to our comfortable lodgings the daily routines of our domestic life changed immeasurably, focused naturally on the needs of the baby who guzzled gallons from his mother's breast, slept interminably – except for a feed at two or three in the morning – and filled Terry-towelling nappies at an unseemly rate of turnover.

Changing nappies was mostly fun, even though the tiny person's arms and legs were throwing punches or kicking for goal. Wielding the huge safety pins required dextrous fingers and utter

Alan with baby Denis

concentration. Washing nappies, however, was a tiresome chore ... no washing machine but a scrubbing board, a large bar of soap, action in the kitchen sink before boiling the bulky towelling in a huge saucepan on the gas stove. Drying depended on the weather: outdoors on warm or windy days, otherwise indoors on the multi-railed rack attached to the kitchen ceiling, lowered and raised by a rope-and-pulley system. Yes, a tiresome daily operation mainly carried out by Betty but shared when I was home.

During those first days of fatherhood I was still engrossed in a labour of love in the County Ground library. I was also searching for a job in Southampton and was about to accept the offer of a boring position in a warehouse, packing and addressing boxes of electric light bulbs, when the Skipper bounded into the library, waving a piece of paper and exclaiming, "Rex Chester has offered you a job at Warnford."

Rex Chester, he explained, was a wealthy businessman who owned a large agricultural estate in the Meon Valley. He was a member of the Hampshire committee and was looking for somebody to work in the estate office.

"Let me know if you are interested," Desmond Eagar said, "and I will arrange a meeting with Major Hurst who runs the estate office."

That evening Betty and I discussed the offer. We agreed that we desperately needed additional income but, having looked up Warnford on the map, we were concerned about the distance. We reckoned it was twenty miles on a bus. After a long chat we agreed that I should meet with Major Hurst.

We were experiencing a period of transitions – the near future uncertain – but in those weeks of autumn '49 I enjoyed being a student librarian and an apprentice dad ... books and nappies! Today I am surrounded by books but there's not a nappy in sight!

The journey to Warnford involved a bus from home to the Civic Centre, then an 80-minute ride on the Hants and Dorset number 55, a green double-decker bus. The return fare to the George Inn at Warnford was four shillings and two pence – more than a pound for a five-day week.

The Estate Office was a small, pleasant, single-storey building located beside the A32, which was not a busy traffic route in 1949. I knocked on the front door and entered. Major Hurst rose from his desk and greeted me with a firm handshake, called me Alan and said, "I'm Ken Hurst, known around here as Major Hurst ... but please call me Ken."

I immediately sensed a warm, kind and efficient personality. All my doubts and questions about 'would I like him? ... could I work under an authoritarian army major?' dissipated within the first few minutes. We chatted about cricket for a while, Ken revealing that he was a keen follower of the Hampshire team.

The boss, Mr RP Chester, was not only a passionate Hampshire supporter and committeeman but also Chairman of Portsmouth FC and a keen golfer. His son, also named Rex, was fourteen, a border at Winchester College, a keen cricketer and all-round sportsman.

Before the war the 2,000-acre estate had been the second largest pig farm in Europe, but it was now mostly dairy farming – 500 head of Shorthorns and Guernseys – as well as a few sows, some arable farming, shooting and woodland. The job was to manage the wages for the 42 employees, to maintain the milking records for the three dairies and to undertake some filing and typing. The working hours, determined by the bus timetable, would be 9.20 to 4.40, and the wages £5 a week with no deductions as the County Club were still Alan's main employer.

"I expect I'll sometimes need your help on the estate," the major added. "It's a big farm. Oh, and of course I must take you to the indoor cricket net that RP has set up for young Rex and his friends. I think RP expects you to do some coaching in the school holidays."

With this all explained, they set off on a tour of the farm.

> I felt 'at home' … strangely … surprisingly. But at the time I did not understand 'why', and I always needed to 'try to understand', even in childhood. The pungent aromas in and around the dairy reminded me of happy holidays at Uncle Charles' farm in Suffolk; the variegated colours of undulating fields ploughed brown or reflecting shades of pasture green; the autumn-leaved trees, winding hedgerows and the livestock … cows, cows and cattle … and more cows stimulated within me a 'oneness' with the environment. Those thoughts and feelings were enhanced by a visit to the indoor cricket net which was in a disused pig house. A rustic contrast to Alf Gover's cricket school in Wandsworth.

A warm cup of tea and more discussion back in the Estate Office led me to accept the job. I agreed to start the next Monday and to stay till the end of March, at which point we shook hands and I caught the bus home.

Betty was delighted that I had accepted the job and relieved that we would no longer have money worries. She had readily adjusted to the routines of motherhood, enjoyed her new role and was very proud to be 'a mother'. Denis was healthy, lively and loud!

We visited our parents, family and friends in London at Christmas and moved to 46 St James Road, Shirley in February, renting two rooms and sharing the kitchen and bathroom. The landlady, Mrs Hunt, was a kindly young widow bringing up two daughters, aged ten and eight. A qualified nurse, she worked part-time at the nearby General Hospital and occasionally looked after Denis in the evenings so that we could go dancing or to a social function. During that winter we became friends with Harold and Elizabeth Webb who ran Southampton's premier school of ballroom dancing in the annexe of a large house in Bassett Avenue; they also gave exhibitions at dinner dances and civic functions at the Guildhall.

The other activity that winter for Alan, one of which he retained very few memories, was football. As a seventeen-year-old he had played for Tottenham Hotspur Juniors when Joe Hulme was manager. By 1949 Hulme had been replaced by Arthur Rowe, but he thinks that it was probably Hulme who brought his name to the attention of Southampton FC.

> I was invited to train at the Dell one evening a week, with the squad that made up the 'A' and 'B' teams, but I opted out soon after starting the job at Warnford. I played a few games with the 'B' team, two at the Dell, and was then referred to Winchester FC for whom I played at inside-left.
>
> I have no 'picture memory' of games I played that winter or of team members, but I do have powerful recall of the cold upper deck of the Hants and Dorset buses on which I travelled to Warnford and back that winter. Reading or writing was almost impossible, but the views were enjoyable and educational when it wasn't raining, which it did a lot. I became an accomplished dozer!
>
> So 'Junior', the young cricketer, experienced a winter of buses and cows, of rain, mud and cold hands, a working environment that I enjoyed, a home life that was happy and an apprenticeship in parenting for Betty and me. We were solvent, had time to meet new friends and take a glimpse at the local dancing scene.
>
> At Warnford I met people I respected and liked. I experienced, once again, that the love of cricket and the respect between cricketers at all levels of the sport removed social boundaries and opened doors to opportunity and friendship. At Warnford I felt at home though 'home' was a long way away!

5

Who will bat at number three?
Summer 1950

After a winter of buses, cows and nappies, Alan returned to the County Ground in good heart. Friendships were renewed and newcomers welcomed.

Derek Shackleton and Cliff Walker were now in The Hutch, among the capped players whose ranks had been depleted by the retirements of veterans George Heath and Lofty Herman, both now licensees of public houses, and Jim Bailey who was working for one of Rex Chester's companies. Also gone from The Hutch was the Yorkshireman Gilbert 'Dinty' Dawson, who had scored more than 1,000 runs in each of the last two summers but whose social manners did not quite fit into the kind of team Desmond Eagar and the senior players wanted Hampshire to be.

> The older players had lost mates; the younger ones glimpsed opportunities; we all lost the presence of matchless characters.

The process of rebuilding the team was well under way. Most pressing was the need for a bowler to take the new ball with Derek Shackleton and, with no obvious candidate among the younger players, the county had recruited the 31-year-old Vic Cannings, who had failed to establish himself as a regular first-teamer at Warwickshire. Fortuitously Cannings had made a rare appearance the previous August against Hampshire at Edgbaston, where his medium-pace out-swingers impressed Neville Rogers and Neil McCorkell. When they discovered that he was Hampshire born, they urged Desmond Eagar to sign him – and thus began a partnership, Shackleton and Cannings, that soon became a byword throughout the county circuit for relentless, nagging accuracy.

Of more significance to Alan was the gap in the batting line-up that was left by the departure of Gilbert Dawson. Amid the banter and the debates in the uncapped players' Black Hole the question was asked, "Who will bat at number three?"

> Neil McCorkell and Neville Rogers were our established and successful opening batsmen, and Johnny Arnold anchored the

batting at number four. Cliff Walker had scored 1,087 runs in his debut season but was disinclined to bat at number three. All-rounder Gerry Hill had batted from numbers one to eleven in his long career but was more suited to batting at six or seven.

My intuition nudges me to suspect that the experienced cricketers on the Selection Committee – Desmond Eagar, Charlie Knott and Cecil Paris – were probably long in debate but short of an easy answer to the question: 'Who will bat at number three?'

Among the youngsters the two most likely candidates to fill the gap were Alan and Hampshire-born Jimmy Gray, who was two years older than Alan and was entering his fourth year on the county staff.

Jimmy was a determined professional in mind and practice, interested in statistics and averages. I was a hybrid amateur-professional and had rejected averages since I was fourteen when playing in five different teams, men and boys, had caused too many mathematical complications. I would bat at any number if I could score enough runs to be awarded my Hampshire cap. That was my only ambition at that time.

Jimmy scored consistently in the 2nd XI, displayed a good defensive technique and concentration, took wickets bowling slow-medium in-swingers and was an excellent fielder in the slips and outfield. He was a prime candidate for Desmond Eagar's new-generation team.

While the question was not uppermost in Alan's thoughts, it was one he explored with fascination while writing this book, even plunging into the statistics of that summer. He did this while England wrestled with the same problem, debating the pros and cons of Joe Root batting at number three.

I find it fascinating that, as I research material for this book, I am discovering facts and patterns of which I was totally unaware, ignored or avoided when playing.

The role of a number three batsman is polymorphic. Basically he needs to be a tough and patient character, possessing a skilled and proven defensive technique, able to replace an opening batsman out for a low score to a fast bowler fired up by his success. He also needs to be an attacking strokemaker able to maintain, even increase, the run rate following an opening partnership of 100 or more ... plus every situation in between.

The man who would turn out to be the county's solution to this question, Henry Horton, was not on the staff in 1950, but followers of Southampton football would have seen him during the winter, playing at wing half for Blackburn Rovers. In the previous four summers he had played 11 matches for Worcestershire but, with an average of 8 with the bat, he had been discarded as simply not good enough.

One of county cricket's most prolific run-scorers, culminating in the golden summer of 1961 when his 2,329 runs were crucial in Hampshire's first championship title, Horton would probably never have played another first-class match if he had not been transferred from Blackburn to Southampton and if Arthur Holt had not invited him in May 1953 to turn out for the county in a two-day friendly against the Army. Such are the quirks of fate in sport … and, of course, life.

In 1950 Hampshire tried eight different batsmen at number three, and the statistics, carefully analysed by Alan, make sorry reading. There were 31 fixtures in the season, and after 30 of them the number three slot had yielded just two fifties. Jimmy Gray, Gerry Hill, Leo Harrison, Cliff Walker, Desmond Eagar, David Blake, the Reverend John Bridger and finally Alan were each given a turn at number three, and their combined tally of 866 runs was at an average of barely 16.

With just one fixture left in the summer, there was no solution in sight.

*

The season started with a friendly against Sussex, a match scheduled for two days. The first was lost to snow, the second played in bitterly cold conditions.

> Hands in pockets were permitted – really? yes, really – by the authority of the captain, Mr Desmond Eagar. No scorecard is available from any source to check bowling stats … maybe the scorer's hands were too numb to create a legible scorebook or the printer had seized up.
>
> Never mind the scorer's hands. How about the bowlers? I clearly remember that our new member of staff, Flight-Lieutenant Alec Debnam, who had been Kent's understudy for England's Doug Wright, sprayed leg-spinners out of reach of the batsmen, even over their heads. Embarrassing! Non-bowlers were sympathetic, seam bowlers erratic and grumpy, Alec despondent.
>
> Vic Cannings shared the cold ball with Shack on that freezing Thursday. Some character! Hampshire born, a very good cricketer, card player and raconteur.

Vic Cannings and Derek Shackleton

From a dearth of fit seam bowlers we now had five: Shackleton, Cannnings, Carty, Walker and Gray, three of whom could be classified as all-rounders. 27-year old Dick Carty, a local lad who traded as a panel-beater, was spotted by Arthur Holt playing cricket in Southampton's parks. He was quick but prone to injury; when fit and on full throttle, he was one of very few really quick English bowlers playing at that time.

I was twelfth man for our first match, and Dick's pace was comparable with Warwickshire's Tom Pritchard, a New Zealander who was considered to be the fastest bowler on the county circuit.

Alan came into the eleven for the next match at Lord's. This was his first appearance for Hampshire at the ground he loved so much, and it was a mystery to him that he retained no memory of the occasion, especially as he batted with some success, scoring 29 against his great Finchley friend Ian Bedford, best man at his wedding. Rain washed out the first two days, but the third day was significant for being the first appearance of Vic Cannings.

That Shack and Vic birthed their partnership on the historic greensward of Lord's gives me goose-bumps. That I fielded at mid-off and witnessed, close up, the new partnership annihilate the first six Middlesex batsmen, including the Great Quartet of Robertson, Brown, Edrich and Compton, is giving me double goose-bumps as I type.

	O	M	R	W
Shackleton	15	0	57	3
Cannings	17	7	21	3

Now in his third season Derek was establishing a reputation as one of the most, if not the most, economical seam-swing bowlers on the county circuit. That being so, the figures above attest to a triumphant Hampshire debut for Vic: seven maidens for Vic, none for Derek! And among his victims: *DCS Compton b Cannings 4*. The first of many victories for Vic.

"Compo was my rabbit," he always claimed in later years.

While the Hampshire team travelled west to Oxford, Alan was despatched to the 2nd XI in Bristol where he scored a century against a Gloucestershire attack that included the future England off-spinner John Mortimore.

In his six 2nd XI games that summer Alan averaged 51, in marked contrast to Jimmy Gray's 20. Yet the only memory he records of those matches was of a bizarre moment before the game at Broadstairs when he and Alec Debnam strolled out to look at the pitch, only to discover that the white lines at the two ends were painted on adjoining wickets.

After a run of good scores, Alan was given a non-championship game at Cambridge, when Shackleton, Cannings, Walker and Eagar were all rested.

Cambridge University cricket was exceptionally strong. The best schoolboy sportsmen could win places without top academic records and, having completed two years of National Service, they were mature young men. With the Fenner's square as true as any in the country, their batting was especially strong. The first three – David Sheppard, John Dewes and Hubert Doggart – would all play for England that summer, and number four, Peter May, would follow the next year. Three weeks earlier, against the touring West Indians, they had scored 594 for four, and by the end of the first day against Hampshire they had reached 409 for two, with Peter May on 202 not out.

It was the only time Alan played at Cambridge, and the match left a lasting mark on him. He knew enough to appreciate the role of Cambridge in cricket history – from the Honourable Ivo Bligh, Ranjitsinhji and Gilbert

Jessop in Victorian times to the England captains Walter Robins and Gubby Allen for whom he had played. In his National Service days he had been skippered by the much admired Squadron-Leader Alan Shirreff, whom he could feel had 'a mysterious *something* I did not have in my life'.

> Given my social background and grammar school education in wartime London, 'Cambridge' had always symbolised something lofty and mysterious, academically out of reach yet desirable.
>
> Although articulate and a thinker I was neither knowledgeable nor studious. I was a communicator and socially confident, played cricket more by instinct and talent than theory. Later, I realised that the *something missing* I had associated with Cambridge had been an unconscious yearning for academic study in an environment of beauty and excellence. I realise now that I was blessed on that glorious summer's day in 1950 with a glimpse of a mysterious grace.
>
> I became fully immersed in the game, in the surrounding environment, in the graceful athleticism and performance art of the players around me ... yet at times I was momentarily 'lost' in the history of cricket and cricketers at the ground ... the achievements of former Blues ... the past merging with the present to the extent that there were moments when I felt I was floating within a bubble of joy – *a cocoon of beauty and excellence.*
>
> At the same time I was grounded in the 'here and now': busy all day – very busy – sharing duties at cover point with Johnny Arnold, mentally analysing the batsmen's styles and tactics, physically quick off the mark to prevent singles and the ever hoped-for run-out. So many balls beat me to the boundary, but I chased them all in support of team-mate bowlers trying hard to maintain line and length in the hope of stemming the avalanche of runs flowing from the bats of John Dewes and Peter May.
>
> Students? They were young masters of the art of batting.

His recall of this 'cricket heaven' was mixed with an awareness that he was excluded from it, in no small measure by the English class system. The world around them was changing, with a Labour government in power. Some of the Hampshire team, Alan himself sometimes, voted Labour.

> In 1950 'Cambridge Blue' symbolised the practice of playing first-class cricket as an amateur, a social status above that of players such as Hutton, Compton, Evans and Bedser, who ranked as low-paid

professionals. In Britain, however, social, economic and cultural upheavals that evolved during and after the war had begun to loosen opinions and modernise traditional practices in the cricket world.

For example, in contrast to pre-war norms, Hampshire's Oxford Blue captain, Desmond Eagar, had decreed that amateur and professional team members should stay in the same hotels and use the same dressing rooms. In my experience relationships with our amateurs David Blake, Vic Ransom, John Bridger and Charlie Knott were always friendly and the social atmosphere comfortable.

At Fenner's Alan was conscious that it was somewhat different.

The players and members of Cambridge University Cricket Club were friendly enough, but the overall social atmosphere in and around the pavilion and on the playing field contrasted significantly with that experienced in county championship matches.

The student cricketers were a talented collective, youthful, bursting with high confidence and physical energy. Several high achievers were already England cricketers or soon to be. 'Not to be' was never contemplated.

On the second day, after the students had declared on 467 for four, it was the turn of the Hampshire batsmen to enjoy the still perfect pitch.

In sublime weather our three senior professionals – Neil McCorkell, Johnny Arnold and Gerry Hill – stroked the ball with veteran grace through gaps in the field, as though playing in a Southampton park on a Sunday afternoon. Johnny had made his debut for Hampshire in 1929, Gerry and Neil three years later. The war had bitten six years from their careers, and now they were enjoying their twilight days, relieved of ambition to play for England or top the averages.

In contrast, the life-goals of the fresh-faced Cambridge bowlers and fielders were embryonic and yet to be tested in whatever career path they chose. That the Young Gentlemen were already ahead of me in 'the game of life' was plainly obvious.

Hampshire finished the match on 435 for nine, 32 runs short of the Cambridge score. Alan himself went to the wicket at 182 for four.

I took guard from Frank Lee, looked round at the field placings and felt confident that I could bat freely and make fifty or more. Not only was the pitch unfriendly to the bowlers, but the Cambridge skipper, Tony Rimmel, was bowling non-turning off-spinners from one end and giving all the non-bowlers a turn at the other. I hit ten off one over, then a four, then waited while a sub-committee of intellectuals debated the preferred field placements for the next non-bowler – yet to be identified.

Alan was about to have his first encounter with a man who would play a major part in his future life-story – David Sheppard.

"What does he bowl?' I asked myself. "He's a big strong chap, must be quickish." Wrong: the future bishop placed the bowler's white metal disc three paces behind umpire Ken McCanlis who, displaying a cheeky grin, called down the wicket to me, "Left arm, round the wicket."

The Geminian twins in me started to argue. *'E's a slow tweaker'* … *'Nah, can't be, 'es too stiff. 'E's like a Grenadier Guard outside Buck' Ouse. Tweakers is like cat burglars, small an' supple.'* … *'Wait-n-see!'*

Only the Sheppard head was visible behind and above umpire Ken; then a long arm appeared – was it Sheppard's or Ken's – followed by broad shoulders with legs that stepped three paces. The arm swung high and released the ball, which floated higher ... and oh-so-slowly-slowly ... time enough for the twins to debate: *'Goin' to land short on off stump'* … *'Nah, it's way outside – pull it fer six'* … *'Nah, back defence safer – if it ever arrives.'*

I waited and played back defence … The ball drifted in off the pitch … I played outside the ball which brushed a pad. All eleven posh young men of Cambridge ROARED … flung arms high, opened mouths wide again, then stared at friendly umpire Ken. There was a long silence of maybe five seconds. Ken joined in the theatrics, displayed an even wider grin, waited … then very slowly raised his left arm, stiff and straight from his shoulder as though performing a slow march at the Trooping of the Colour, index finger extended heavenwards. I marched at pace towards the pavilion, cross and muttering inanities.

Alan was the first of only two first-class wickets taken by David Sheppard.

In the late 1960s I spent time with David and his wife, Grace, at the Mayflower Family Centre and never asked about his second victim – but then cricket was not on the agenda.

Alan did not return to Cambridge till 1972, when his son Martin was studying engineering at Jesus College. Alan was well aware of the social and cultural changes of the intervening years and welcomed many of them. His eldest son Denis, a talented sportsman who had been educated at Millfield, had rejected university in favour of the new-age freedom of a hippy musician's life, and Alan himself had trained as a community worker at college in Birmingham. Yet, for all his unease about the old class system and his embrace of change, the contrast between the Cambridge of 1972 and that of 1950 left him troubled.

> When set against my idealised memories of 1950 the changes I witnessed that day in 1972 seemed jaw-droppingly radical! Dress code was now scruffy jeans and t-shirts for both sexes, skirts from minimal to full length: academic gowns, blazers and ties were worn 'in hall' but no longer in the streets, cafes and bars. There were more cycles, more students, more females, more freedoms; there were fewer inhibitions, more snogging in public, more sex in private. Pubs were packed and very noisy; smokers and non-smokers inhaled tobacco smoke and that other sweet-smelling 'stuff'; drunkenness was rife. Of the many new buildings most were vast, efficient and adaptable but unattractive to me.
>
> I remember thinking, as I drove back to London, that, whereas my senses and sensibilities had been inspired by the cultural environment of Cambridge in 1950, today I felt deflated, disappointed ... saddened. The overall social scene had become visibly more materialistic and, to me, seemed to be less academic, less purposeful and bordering on the hedonistic.

However, Alan was sufficiently intelligent to know that these impressions from a day visit were not the whole story.

> Undoubtedly, behind and even within the 'with it' façade, the seriously minded core of academics and students at Cambridge University were breaking barriers and opening pathways in every field of their diverse endeavours.

*

Alan was twelfth man for the match against the tourists, this year the West Indies, who travelled to Southampton from Lord's where, amid the joyous celebration of their supporters, they had gained their first Test victory on English soil. Heroes of the triumph were their two young spinners, Sonny

Ramadhin and Alf Valentine, the latter of whom was Alan's fellow twelfth man. "He was somewhat shy," Alan recalled, "but we got on well."

What a crowd gathered that Saturday morning at Northlands Road! Arriving on his bike at 9.30, he pushed through the slow-moving queue – "Sorry, office staff," he said when they protested, and soon enough he was bowling in the nets to the Hampshire team. He had never before seen so many people around the nets, the 10,000-strong crowd filling the ground to capacity – and more.

> Did our assistant secretary, Colonel Binney, order the gates to be closed? I'm not sure, but I do remember that the boundary rope was repeatedly reduced in circumference before play and again at lunch.

The day was dominated by the batting of Everton Weekes. Already on the tour he had hit a triple century and two doubles, and in four hours of supreme stroke play he dazzled the crowd with an innings of 246 not out.

> His effortless power off the back foot and flowing drives through the covers and wide of mid-on thrilled the spectators. His timing, placement of shots and obvious enjoyment of batting lifted the spirits of everyone privileged to be present. We all became fans of Everton de Courcy Weekes.
>
> In the dressing room at tea-time Neville Rogers quietened the chatter. "Mac has something to say," he said. Our wicket-keeper Neil McCorkell, a wise and modest man, seldom 'spoke to the dressing room' so we all listened keenly. "Well, that Everton Weekes is certainly a fine batsman," he said. "When he was on 80 he square-cut a four and turned to me. 'Maaan,' he said. 'That's the first one I've timed today.'"

In his next match at Leicester Weekes would score another double hundred, but the innings at Southampton that would prove of greater significance was a stylish one of 135, with 14 fours and two sixes, by their opener Roy Marshall, who three years later would join the county. To his regret Alan retained no memory of that innings, though he did have a mind-picture of the powerful Clyde Walcott's 58. The big man had pulled a thigh muscle and was batting with a runner.

> Though injured and almost static, he proceeded to wave his bat at the ball as though swatting flies to their doom – his nonchalant style adding to the plethora of batting delights that day

The Hampshire bowling attack, without Vic Cannings, manfully sent down 142 overs in the 6½-hour day, but they posed few problems. It was only the keen fielding that saved the score from being greater than 539 for four.

Leo Harrison's athletically elegant out-fielding performance, and yes I mean performance, remains crystal clear in my memory. The slim, lithe, blond Leo, a Hampshire man in heart and soul, was a stylish batsman, our reserve wicketkeeper and an outstanding cover-point fielder. Oh, if only I could project the scene in my mind, rapturously appreciated by ten thousand spectators, onto a home-movie screen.

I was sitting on the balcony of The Hutch with veterans Arthur Holt, Jim Bailey and Sam Pothecary. Watching and chatting, we soon realised that Leo was consciously putting on a show and enjoying the applause from his appreciative audience. The 'vets' and I were Leo's most vociferous fans when he was patrolling the third-man boundary in front of us.

Everton Weekes was cutting hard and often, at other times driving to the left of cover or dabbing late cuts. Leo, quick off the mark, left or right, flowing balletic movement, picked up one-hand on the run inches from the rope, lightning stylish throw – thud – the ball in Mac's gloves over the stumps without Mac having to move either way ... time and time again. I am chuckling now and can't help repeating 'brilliant Leo – beautiful memory!' My words will not do justice to this scene that I see again! I admit to being a little jealous.

Some back-foot drives and cuts were not racing towards the boundary but varying in pace over the smooth grass of the outfield. With instinctive timing Leo adjusted his running speed to ensure he met the ball inches before it touched the boundary rope – one-hand pick-up either side, throw, thud into Mac's gloves over the stumps, applause! I write it again: 'time and time again'. Leo, dear team mate, you sure did entertain that great crowd, and your colleagues, that glorious West Indian day in Southampton! Thank you!

Timing, balance, depth of concentration and flow of physical movement are but four of the defining high-level graces that set apart top-echelon athletes who are a delight to watch, who are elegant and graceful, yet also powerful. As individuals we have our favourites. Among mine are Learie Constantine, Tom Graveney, Derek Shackleton, Roger Federer, Martina Navratilova, Ronaldo,

Usain Bolt, Gary Sobers, Denise Lewis, David Gower, Ray Lindwall, Tiger Woods, Roy Marshall and Leo Harrison.

With rain washing out play on Monday, the game did not live up to its glorious Saturday. On Tuesday, on a damp track, Ramadhin spun his mysteries, taking four wickets, and Neville Rogers showed his class with a century.

> Neville batted beautifully and consistently throughout the season. In all, he scored 1,857 runs, including five centuries. His form and exemplary professional manner was noted by the press as a potential candidate for Test selection.

In the three summers from 1950 to 1952 Rogers scored more than 6,000 runs, but he got no closer to England recognition than being named as twelfth man for the final Test of 1951 when Yorkshire's Frank Lowson was preferred to him. Who was the best player of that era who did not play for England? According to Jimmy Gray, "The Surrey players all said it was Neville. There were very few batsmen who could spot Alec Bedser's leg-cutter, it was such a small variation, but Neville did."

In the years that followed, there developed a feeling in the county that the selectors did not favour Hampshire. Not since 1931, when Johnny Arnold was picked for a single Test against New Zealand, had a Hampshire cricketer played for England – and only three would do so before Chris Smith's call-up in 1983. In the 52 years between Arnold's only Test and Smith's first, 265 players represented England in 404 Tests, a total of 4,444 caps, and Hampshire's trio (Shackleton, White and Cottam) contributed just 11 to that total, far below the next lowest county, Glamorgan on 56.

I wonder. Would Neville Rogers, Jimmy Gray or Trevor Jesty have stood more chance if they had played for Surrey, Middlesex or Yorkshire?

*

In the fortnight following the West Indies match, Alan returned to the 2nd XI where he continued to score runs, including an innings of 82 against Middlesex at Basingstoke. The 1st XI went north to Bradford, then to Derby, before having a three-day break. During that brief interlude in the season the lives of three Hampshire cricketers changed course.

First, Derek Shackleton. The top seam bowler in the national averages, he travelled from Derby to spend the weekend with his family in Todmorden, meeting up with his his fiancée Kathy whom he was set to marry in August. Unusually for that time, he had been granted a match off for the wedding – but only one, leaving his honeymoon to play at Eastbourne.

During his weekend in Todmorden he received a telegram, telling him to report to Trent Bridge for the next Test. Taking the new ball with Alec Bedser, he had a tough match as Frank Worrell (261) and Everton Weekes (129) plundered the England bowling, but he had the consolation of top-scoring with 42 in the England first innings, receiving a standing ovation when he returned to the pavilion. He was not retained for the final Test.

While Shack's selection brought joy to his Hampshire team-mates, the news of Johnny Arnold darkened their mood. He was having the best of seasons, in fine form at Bradford where he hit two fifties, but, reporting sick after the match at Derby, he was diagnosed with tuberculosis, entered hospital for treatment and never played again for the county.

> Johnny had been in excellent batting form that season, scoring 1,119 runs in 29 innings at an average of 41.44. A delightful, chirpy and popular man, he had scored over 21,000 runs for Hampshire, including 36 centuries. I had the privilege of batting with him – he was a delight to watch and learn from – and, especially for me, his fielding at cover point was beautiful and inspiring.

The third Hampshire cricketer whose fortunes were changed by that fateful weekend was, of course, Alan. As the in-form batsman in the 2nd XI, it fell to him to grasp the opportunity presented by the departure of Johnny Arnold. There were 13 matches remaining, time enough to make his mark with the bat and, in Arnold's absence, in the covers.

Alan had his share of low scores, as all batsmen did in those days of uncovered pitches, but there were also several highlights. His highest score in 1949 had been 35, but he bettered that with 37 against the slow bowlers of Northamptonshire at Bournemouth, then 48 not out against Derbyshire's testing pace attack at Southampton and 64, his maiden fifty and top score of the innings, against Glamorgan at Swansea.

At Leicester Desmond Eagar broke a finger, putting him out of action for the rest of the summer, but he was ever present during the remaining home games. Against Nottinghamshire at Bournemouth, in the ninth of Alan's 13 matches, the skipper took Alan aside for a chat.

> He praised my fielding and said there was a place in the side for me next season if I continued to develop: "A few more fifties and a first century is now expected from you … The Committee have awarded you a two-year contract, Alan, and I am promoting you to number three for the last four matches."

The first of the four was at Eastbourne. With the Reverend John Bridger opening the innings, Alan went in at 89 for one and scored 31 in a partnership of 100 with Neville Rogers. It was the highest stand of the match, and the value of their runs was clear on the final day when Sussex, set 98 for victory, were bowled out for 38.

Next came Yorkshire at Portsmouth, Alan's first encounter with the White Rose county. They had a formidable bowling attack, with the young Freddie Trueman partnering Alec Coxon, the leading wicket-taker among quick bowlers that summer, supported by the slow left-armer Johnny Wardle and the leg spin of Eddie Leadbeater. In a one-sided game the visitors scored 369 for four, then bowled out Hampshire for 113 and 188.

In the first innings Alan had his off stump knocked back by Trueman for 2, but he fared better second time. Coxon at his best, generating pace and bounce, proved too testing for the Hampshire middle order – Hill 5, Walker 2, Gray 1 – but Alan 'shaped well' against him before being bowled by Eddie Leadbetter for 45.

Coxon, who two weeks earlier had been in the England twelve at The Oval, finished with match figures of 10 for 80 in 50 overs, yet he never played another match in the County Championship. Historians of the White Rose county are still not sure what happened – was it, as rumour has it, a punch thrown at Denis Compton in a festival match? – but the fiery Coxon was not retained by Yorkshire. Settling in the north-east, he never mellowed, even in his eighties being banned from his local pub for starting a fight with the barman. One obituary made reference to his 'extreme political views'.

The third of Alan's four matches at number three, against Glamorgan at Portsmouth, was ruined by rain, with Alan out for only 4. That left him with one more chance – at Dean Park, Bournemouth, against Gloucestershire – to demonstrate that he was the number three the county were looking for.

Stand-in captain Charlie Knott's decision to bowl first did not work out well. On the Saturday Gloucestershire batted without much difficulty to reach 304 for seven. On the Sunday it rained and, after an immediate declaration, the Hampshire batsmen had to struggle on a damp and awkward surface against the off-spin of Tom Goddard, only four weeks from his 50th birthday, and the slow left-arm of Sam Cook.

> Basil Allen, the Gloucestershire captain, gave George Lambert and Ken Graveney a few overs before Tom Goddard and Sam Cook bowled unchanged – 39 overs each – to dismiss us for 133.

Tom Goddard was tall and lean, possessed huge hands and long, strong fingers that made the ball spin prodigiously. Since his debut in 1922 he had taken almost 2,900 first-class wickets. Left-arm finger spinner Sam Cook – known as 'The Tetbury Twirler' – had taken over 100 wickets a season since his debut in 1946.

After Neville's early departure, I joined Neil Mac at the wicket. He encouraged me to focus on defence, to be satisfied with singles and hit the rare loose ball hard. I watched how he played the spinners, and his friendly advice lifted my confidence. Our joint battle intensified my concentration; I was probably 'in the zone', though I knew nothing of that concept until many years later.

When Neil Mac was caught at slip for 46, our partnership had accumulated 84 runs. I battled on – according to the *Bournemouth Echo*, my innings lasted three hours and 55 minutes – before being bowled by Tom Goddard for 58. We followed on and were 34 for one at the close of play – Neville Rogers not out 19, Punchy 15.

Their partnership had reached 70 when Rogers was out for 27. Cliff Walker and Jimmy Gray soon followed before Leo Harrison and Alec Debnam provided some support for Alan, who by mid-afternoon had reached 94, closing in on a maiden century. Then he was deceived by George Lambert's slower ball and was caught and bowled. The match and the season were soon all over, Gloucestershire winning by nine wickets.

In all-out totals of 133 and 188 Alan had scored 58 and 94, batting with assurance in the most testing of conditions for more than seven hours.

> They were two of the best – maybe the best – innings of my ten years as a professional cricketer. George Emmett came into our dressing room to congratulate me; my team mates complimented me in various manners including slaps on the back and "Well played, Punchy!"
>
> Desmond Eagar, Charlie Knott, Neil McCorkell and Neville Rogers had little chats in the dressing room or the bar after changing into civvies. I was too tired for all the attention to swell my ego; I accepted that I had played well for the team and that I might get a duck in the next match – except there was no 'next match'.
>
> That I battled against Goddard and Cook on a turning wicket for a total of seven hours and ten minutes now tests my credulity. That John Arlott witnessed those innings at Dean Park and wrote about them in *The Cricketer* reminds me of the talent I possessed

but failed to develop to its full potential. I did not read the article at that time; when I did, years later, I thought, 'Was that piece really about me?'

Arlott wrote as follows:

> My own most heartening experience of the season has been the batting of Alan Rayment of Hampshire. His first few innings were not numerically impressive and he could probably have benefited by another season with the second eleven. He 'came', however, in the last match of the season, against the severe test of Goddard and Cook, the Gloucester spin bowling combination, on a turning wicket.
>
> With no other Hampshire batsman handling them in either innings, Rayment made fifty in his first 'knock' and was barely short of a century in the second. The wicket favoured the bowlers throughout, yet he never gave a chance. Most impressive of all was the maturity of his method: never once – and I watched him with the utmost care from start to finish of the game – never once did he take a liberty with a good ball or fail to punish a bad one. No matter how good the bowler, if he bowled a bad ball it was hit – hard – and Rayment has attacking strokes all round the wicket. His two innings answered many questions about him and certainly proved the wisdom of his two years' groundwork. He has shown considerable promise.

Arlott returned to Alan in 'Some English Cricket Prospects', the last chapter of his book about the summer, *Days at the Cricket*.

> The two best innings I saw played by a young cricketer in 1950 were those of Rayment for Hampshire against Gloucestershire at Bournemouth ... The entire ground was as disappointed as he was himself at his failure to score his first century. He was easily the outstanding Hampshire batsman of the match. He played the fast bowling of Lambert firmly and the spinners of Cook and Goddard with an air of experience ... He is of the mental calibre to improve by coaching and experience. His stroke-play is varied and well-controlled. It is early yet to prophesy a great future, but certainly no more could be asked of a young man than the two innings he produced at Bournemouth.

In the next paragraph Arlott, not always at his best with a crystal ball, was less enthusiastic about Jimmy Gray.

> He has a sound-looking defence and a pleasing style but so far appears to lack strokes ... If his county can nurse him through a possible spell of low scores, he seems likely to become an extremely solid, sheet-anchor type of middle-order batsman.

In the county's search for a number three, it was Alan who was making the strongest claim.

Alan, batting against Gloucestershire at Bournemouth
'A faultless display, characterised by perfect timing, sound defence and superb driving on both sides of the wicket' – Bournemouth Daily Echo

6

Farm, family and dancing
Winter 1950/51

The summer was over. Hampshire had risen four places to 12th in the 1950 table. *Wisden*, acknowledging the opportunities given to young players, declared that to be 'quite satisfactory', noting Alan's promise and suggesting that he 'looked like the successor to Arnold.'

> Summer to autumn, cricket to farming, hotel rooms to home comforts, organised calendar to self-management – well, shared management with Betty who was energetically creative and efficient in all domestic and motherly aspects of daily living. Denis was no longer a baby-baby but an adventurous crawler, strong in body and determined in mind.
>
> When leaving my job in Warnford in the spring, Major Hurst told me that he and Mr Chester would welcome having me back in the autumn. I replied that I was grateful and would like to return but the journey by bus was onerous. Then I asked, rather cheekily, if Mr Chester would allow me to use one of the cars in the barn opposite Wheely Down House. I believe there were eight of them. To my surprise the answer was yes so on Monday 18 September I boarded a green Hants and Dorset bus, viewed familiar scenes from a front seat, top deck, knowing that I would be returning home in a 1937 Standard Nine automobile, colour mid-blue. Oh the luxury!
>
> On my journeys to and from the Meon Valley I enjoyed so much the colours: the variegated greens, browns and sky blues of those rural Hampshire landscapes. On the farm itself, green pastures and ploughed muddy fields – dark brown or ginger clay – framed by foliage of hedge and tree in autumn hues. Plenty of brown among the yellow straw in the cow barns, accompanied by that unforgettably pungent aroma of manure; also an abundance of brown cow-pats in green grazing fields. Oh! and a favourite sight – a Ferguson tractor painted light and dark green, probably an artistic endeavour by the chauffer Ron Clark.

I loved my job, and I enjoyed the community lifestyle and the warm working relationships; the Major and Ron Clark became friends. I felt at home, though I missed Betty and Denis during the long days of winter.

I well remember the net practice in the converted pig barn with young Rex and his friend Peter Short; a lunch at Wheely Down House, attended by the majority of Hampshire's first-team players, and, most of all, Billy the Bull.

A veterinary team were assembled in the relatively tall boar house of the largest piggery to examine the pregnancy of cows and heifers. Billy, a young bull who was running with the herd, was in the single-line queue of cows progressing slowly along the narrow central aisle, bordered by pig pen walls and iron rails – and Billy was being obstreperous. Colonel Locke the manager, positioned by the boar house some thirty feet from my safe perch on a piggery wall, shouted, "Rayment, get that bull under control!"

I grabbed a handy broom, cautiously eased over a rail into the aisle, proffered the broom towards Billy's ringed nose, wet and snorting, and commanded, "Back there, Billy … Go-o-o on … Back there, boy!" I was scared shitless but maintained a strong voice – and Billy obliged. After about four minutes the queue moved forward, and a cowman took charge of Billy. Phew!

At home, exclamations of 'gee', 'well done' and even 'trriffic' were encouragements for Denis the crawler when playing with wooden building bricks, dinky motor cars, drawing and being read to by Betty or myself. Low-level cupboards had to be emptied or locked, overhanging table cloths removed following a crockery disaster, and painting with watercolours supervised to prevent pop-art on walls and carpets.

I still have the mind-video of Denis's first solo walk on his first birthday. Grandma Wyn held his hand outside the front door of our house; I was squatting by the front gate twenty feet away, saying softly, 'Come on, Denis … Walk to Daddy.' And he did, with a really determined facial expression, Grandma close behind in case!

Bob Holmes visited later that autumn and, on a pleasant sunny Sunday, drove us through winding secondary roads in the New Forest towards Mudeford. Passing a small farm, Denis, who was sitting on my lap in the back of the Austin Ten, pointed his finger at something in the distance and said, confidently, "Towh", sounding like 'cow' with a 't' instead of a 'c'. Bob and Betty discussed excitedly, "What does he mean? What is a 'towh'? A pause, then as we passed fields where lots of horses were grazing, Denis became very excited again, pointed at the horses and kept saying "Towh ... TOWH." Yes, we got it! Any animal on four legs was a 'TOWH'.

Betty and I were proud of our son's development: solo walk on first birthday, first word a few weeks later and, to top all that, potty-trained the same month.

Alan played his second winter of football, again for Winchester City where Vic Cannings joined him: Vic at right back, Alan at left half. Alan's main memory of the soccer was of the day when he waited for the team coach outside the wrong pub, causing an away match to start an hour late.

Ten minutes, fifteen minutes late – I kept looking for the coach and at my watch, then quickened my pace as I walked, anxiously, up and down the pavement outside the pub. Twenty five, thirty minutes – I had stopped walking in an attempt to calm myself down when I heard a familiar voice shouting, "PUNCHY ... PUNCHY!!"

On a street corner fifty yards away Vic was waving his arms and booming instructions in a voice worthy of a Company Sergeant-Major: "Where have you been, you idiot?" A typical Cannings remark.

The coach driver wound his way through the suburban streets to link up with the eastbound A27, through Fareham to Gosport and across Portsmouth Harbour onto the ferry. Yes, we were playing on the Isle of Wight. The kick-off would definitely be late!

The football came to an end that winter. Not so, the dancing.

Our landlady, Mrs Hunt, kindly offered to care for Denis so that Betty and I could attend the Harold Webb School of Dancing in Bassett Avenue on Saturday evenings, arriving at seven o'clock for an advanced lesson followed by a social dance at eight. We had missed the exercise, fun and friendships of the ballroom world, and we raised our performance standard, becoming friendly with Mrs Elizabeth Webb, a college graduate and dance teacher.

Driving to Warnford one morning in November, I had a 'thought'. Betty and I were qualified teachers; we could start some ballroom dance classes in Shirley. The hall of our local church, St James, was available on Monday evenings from January, and the vicar agreed to hire it to us from 8 to 10 each week, at ten shillings an hour.

In December I placed two double-column display advertisements in the *Southern Echo*, headed ALAN RAYMENT SCHOOL OF DANCING, also one in the parish magazine, a hand-printed poster on the church's notice board and another in the window of the local newsagent. The standard fee for a two-hour beginner's class was 2/6d so we would need eight people just to cover the cost of the hall.

Would anybody attend? Yes – thankfully! Twelve attended the first class. Our gross income from the classes was £21, enough to pay not only for the hall but for a dozen records and a portable gramophone.

Betty and I were determined to succeed in teaching our pupils 'to get round the floor' in the waltz and quickstep and to create a friendly social atmosphere. That we succeeded could be measured by the number who started in January and attended all the classes through to March. Several of them asked for private lessons.

"Are you going to have classes after the cricket season?" many asked. We debated the same question. We had had a busy winter but could not commit to setting up a school of dancing until I had established a regular place in the Hampshire team.

Betty and Alan leading a dance class in 1952 or 1953

7

A fateful stroll around the ground
Summer 1951 and Winter 1951/52

In late March ballroom dance classes gave way to cricket coaching during Hampshire's Easter scheme. As an outgoing personality, young at heart, Alan was a natural with the children.

> As the opening act of a new cricket season, coaching holidaying schoolboys was always a delight. Whether or not a youngster had a smidgen of talent we the professionals, led by Arthur Holt, made sure the boys of all ages had fun. Naturally some were in awe of Derek Shackleton, resplendent in his England blazer, others cheekily confident enough to hit my leg-spinners to the far corners of the nursery ground.
>
> Returning to the County Ground and the world of cricket required major adjustments to daily life for all the playing staff. Several were professional footballers; some had winter jobs at Price's Bakery in Eastleigh or worked in offices near their homes. Cliff Walker returned to Southampton from the family cinema business in Yorkshire, and Punchy changed muddy farm boots and patent dancing shoes for spiked cricket boots. Three of the Hampshire players – Neville Rogers, Leo Harrison and Neil McCorkell – coached in the sunny climes of the southern hemisphere.
>
> The professional staff were a cheerful bunch of sportsmen, and I certainly looked forward to the noisy banter of the group and quiet chats about winter jobs and family life with Cliff Walker, Alec Debnam and Dick Carty. I had remembered the warm greetings and friendly joshing at the beginning of the previous season and now, probably due to my performance at the end of last season, I seemed to be accepted as a member of the first-team squad, though I was yet to win my county cap. There was, of course, due respect from the uncapped group towards the senior players who inhabited The Hutch; we all aspired to have our own bench locker there someday.

Alan at Easter coaching in Southampton in the mid-1950s

Our Black Hole dressing room under the Ladies Stand was seriously overcrowded, with a mixture of youngsters and others of us who had played first-team cricket. We all needed to 'move up' in the next two seasons or we would be 'out' and looking for a new job.

Interesting! Having written 'move up' or 'out' in May 2020, I realise that in April 1951 my mind would not have analysed the uncapped staff situation like that. I may have joked "No more room in this bus, mate!" but nothing more.

My mindset was positive and hopeful. Beloved Arden Field and the Finchley Club, my alma mater, and Lord's, my cathedral, had infused me with confidence twinned with an innocent naivety. Now, at the beginning of my third season at Hampshire, I was so enjoying the fulfilment of 'my dream' to be a county cricketer that I was not at all anxious about the future.

However, as a husband and father I was aware of my serious responsibilities as the breadwinner for our family – and Life was about to challenge my easy-going trust in the people around me.

Though Alan may not have seen it this way, he and Jimmy Gray were in competition for what might be only one place, and at the end of 1950 Alan, the younger by two years, had clearly moved ahead of his rival. Both were good fielders and Jimmy could bowl useful medium-pace, but in both the 1st and 2nd XI Alan had been much the greater run-scorer. With John Arlott's ringing endorsement he had every reason to believe he would start the season in the team.

A further factor in the selectors' mind was that Neil McCorkell, in his 40th year, was retiring at the end of the summer. The plan was for Leo Harrison to take over behind the stumps and, with that in mind and with Harrison's eyesight problems finally sorted out, they were keen to build up his experience with a good run in the side.

On Monday 1 May, ahead of the opening first-class fixture on Saturday, they travelled by coach to Hove to play a two-day friendly against Sussex. Batting first, they were all out for 263, with Alan at number three bowled for 4 and Jimmy Gray and Leo Harrison, down the order, making 59 and 41. In the second innings, they struggled in difficult conditions to 61 for seven off 41 overs. Alan, though top-scoring, failed a second time, bowled for 14.

Then it was back to Southampton for two days of nets before the team took the train to Peterborough on Friday.

The weather on Thursday morning was overcast, following early morning rain, but the net pitches were dry enough for practice by mid-afternoon. Having batted for twenty minutes, I was wirh Reg Dare and Alec Debnam, practising my often wayward leggies on Cliff Walker when Arthur Holt tapped me on the shoulder.

"The Chairman would like a word with you," he said.

"Me, Arthur? What's it about?"

Arthur did not reply but said, "He's coming over now."

Mr WJ Arnold, a director of the builder's merchants Travis & Arnold (later merged with Sandell Perkins to become Travis Perkins), had been elected chairman of the county club in 1950. He had not played first-class cricket and, although we, the players, had been introduced to him during the previous season, I had had no subsequent contact with him. To me he was an almost invisible first officer of the Hampshire Cricket Committee.

Arthur introduced me and, noticeably, disengaged quickly and headed towards the nets.

Mr Arnold said, "Let's go for a stroll round the ground, Alan."

Now I knew that something serious was afoot.

The chairman addressed me in a quiet and almost apologetic manner: "Alan, from your achievements at the end of last season, the selectors believe that you have the talent and character to establish a permanent place in the first team and gain your county cap. However, both Jimmy Gray and Leo Harrison had a disappointing season. As reserve keeper, and with McCorkell retiring, Harrison needs to be playing and scoring runs to boost his confidence, and Gray needs to prove his obvious talent. We have therefore decided that he will bat at number six for the first half of the season. We are not able to include all of you and Gray and Harrison in the team now, Alan, but we do guarantee you a place in the second half of the season. I hope you understand the situation."

Understand? NO! But I had been brought up to be polite and to accept the decisions of authority figures without question.

"Yes, Mr Arnold, I realise that I am younger than Jimmy, and I suppose it is fair that the selectors have allocated half a season to each of us."

The stroll had reached the Ladies Stand, and I peeled off to take refuge in the Black Hole. It was occupied so I went upstairs to enjoy the panoramic view of the ground and to have a think. 'Well, I'll have to wait! I'll enjoy playing in the second team and with the Club & Ground. I'll aim to score lots of runs to embarrass the selectors and maybe take a few wickets.'

"Are you alright, Alan?" Alec Debnam asked when we were changing into day clothes late that afternoon. "You seem to be very quiet." Good friend, Alec, but I replied, "I'm OK, Alec – just having a think about home and what Betty will cook for supper."

After playing with Denis and reading a bedtime story I shared my news with Betty. "Of course I am disappointed, but I do have a two-year contract. We will just have to see how this season goes."

"That's it, Alan. You have two summers to make a breakthrough, and I'm sure you'll get a winter job. We can also set up some more dancing classes in the autumn."

Betty, a practical Taurean, was always concerned about economic stability whereas I had a confidence – a 'something' deep inside me – that trusted Life and the future. In that period of my career I had no thoughts of *not* playing county cricket and, if Hampshire did not retain me, my sub-conscious *knew* I could earn money by coaching cricket, teaching ballroom dancing, keeping accounts and typing letters, decorating and carpentry or even driving a delivery van.

Before breakfast the next morning I walked to the local newsagent, bought a *Daily Telegraph* and had just crossed St James' Road when I stood stock still, my mind struck by a BIG THOUGHT: 'WHY did Mr Arnold, a stranger, break the news to me? WHY NOT the Skipper, Desmond Eagar ... or the coach Arthur Holt ... or Cecil Paris who chaired the Selection Committee ... or Charlie Knott ... ???'

With hindsight, looking at the subsequent careers of Jimmy Gray and Alan, it is hard to conclude that the county made the wrong decision. But in that moment that was unknown. For Alan it was a knock backwards and, though he never saw it this way, it damaged the momentum of his progress and could well have affected his deep-down confidence.

*

It was thirty years later when Alan finally lived through the full emotional impact of that conversation with Mr Arnold.

From 1967 to 1969 Alan studied to be a community worker at Westhill College, a part of the University of Birmingham. Included in the programme of study was a training in counselling, which Alan pursued further after he left Birmingham. In London he joined an evening class run by the Clinical Theology Association (now known as the Bridge Pastoral Foundation), a pioneering group set up to introduce a theological dimension into pyschotherapy and counselling. In the years that followed he became heavily involved in its work, attending many personal growth workshops and undertaking a training in Primal Integration Therapy.

They ran a five-day annual conference, with workshops, at the University of Nottingham, which Alan attended several times. It was during a session in the 1981 conference that Alan relived that afternoon at Northlands Road.

> In mixed groups of ten to fourteen members led by a senior therapist, we discussed and practised primal integration therapy. During the last session our group leader/therapist, the Reverend Jim, turned to me and said, "Alan, you have not done any 'work' this week" – meaning I had not shared a personal problem with the group that might benefit from regression to an earlier time in my life.
>
> I replied, "Jim, over many years I have received a lot of very helpful therapy that has cleared debris from my divorce and career path issues. I can't think of anything to investigate."
>
> Jim, a sports enthusiast, replied, "How about your cricket career that you ended so abruptly. Any regrets?"
>
> "No, I've dealt with that – cleared out all that stuff!"
>
> "Well, be a sport and have a go."
>
> I lay on my back on the floor mat; hands were placed gently on my ankles, arms and head, Jim's soft baritone voice stilled and focused our energies and relaxed my muscles from toe to head. Then, still awake, Jim regressed me to a deeper level of my conscious – back past my summer coaching at Lord's in '59, back past my last season playing for Hampshire and resignation in '58 ... back ... back ... *back to April 1951 ... The Stroll .... The Chairman ... The Rejection.* WHAM!!!
>
> Akin to flipping the safety valve of a pressure cooker, thirty years of repressed negative energy was unleashed and spewed through my mouth in a torrent of loud expletives, accompanied by clenched fists slamming my thighs. My innocent colleagues in the therapy group were the recipients of my long-suppressed anger towards the

Hampshire selection committee of 1951 – and indeed towards Mr Arnold, who did not deserve my resurrected wrath.

I stood up and paced the room, shouting and swearing and pumping fist into palm, slowly calming myself until I was safe to hug and to be consoled by the caring, lovely people around me.

"You never know you know," quipped Jim, who suggested I relate the back story to group colleagues. "Fifteen minutes, Alan, to paint the picture and help us learn something from your experience. Then we must move on – we have time for one more regression before we say our farewells."

Driving home to Brighton that evening I felt calm and happy, refreshed in body, mind and spirit. *Now I understand ... Thank God!*

*

With Neil McCorkell injured in the first match, Alan was back in the team almost immediately, but he did not have a good summer. While Jimmy Gray and Leo Harrison established themselves, each passing 1,000 runs and winning their county caps, Alan struggled.

He stayed in the team for a run of 15 matches, batting mostly at number three, but his 26 innings produced a meagre 409 runs, with 14 single-figure scores and just two fifties: 51 at the Wagon Works ground in Gloucester and 59 against Lancashire at Portsmouth. In the first of these he shared in a century partnership with Neil McCorkill, whose 203 was the highest score of his career, and in the second a century partnership with Neville Rogers. They were special moments in a spell that tested his cheerful spirit.

Alan recorded only two memories of those two months. The first came in the Whit Bank Holiday fixture against Kent at Southampton. Facing a new over from the England leg-spinner Doug Wright, he stepped away to leg in protest at the 'squawking' of Godfrey Evans behind the stumps.

"What the #### are you doing, young Rayment?" Godfrey said.

"I'll bat when you stop your noisy chattering, Godfrey," I replied.

It happened a second time, Evans' noise only stopping when the Kent captain spoke to him. It was a story Alan often told, one of which he was proud, and it demonstrated to him that he had developed since the day when Charlie Harris's mind-games got the better of him.

In my mind I was proud to be a professional cricketer – but in my heart? I think not. Patterns of learned behaviour were embedded in my character. From childhood to adulthood at Finchley Cricket

Club, with the RAF and the Middlesex 2nd XI, my status and mindset was that of a club cricketer, an amateur.

For Hampshire at Southampton in 1949 I had behaved as a professional when I deferred to Charlie Harris, but I regretted that I had not hit that ball for six. Lesson learned, I now felt free to be me!

His second memory was of a catch at Chesterfield, the most memorable of his career, when he shot up a hand at cover point and found to his amazement that the hard-hit ball had stuck in it.

Skipper and team mates gathered round, some laughing, some shaking their heads. Leo Harrison grinned at me: "You looked like that bleedin' statue in New York harbour – only needed a torch."

The Hampshire team at Dudley, June 1951
Standing: Alan Rayment, Jimmy Gray, Cliff Walker, Derek Shackleton, Len Sprankling, Vic Cannings, Reg Dare (twelfth man), Leo Harrison
Seated: Gerry Hill, Charlie Knott, Desmond Eagar, Neil McCorkell, Neville Rogers

In this match Alan caught and bowled Reg Perks. Perks was hardly a prize scalp – he scored more ducks (156) than anybody in the history of first-class cricket – but his dismissal was special to Alan, the first of his 19 first-class wickets.

Alan's run in the team came to an end in early July.

In the nets at headquarters Arthur Holt endeavoured to lift my confidence by his words and deeds, 'throwing down' half-volleys and long hops for me to belt into the netting, his words encouraging and fatherly. I doubt that anyone at Northlands Road knew about therapists and counselling in 1951, but Arthur was a good listener, patient and empathetic. He made no mention of the chairman's 'stroll and chat' in April, but I think he knew more than I did how that news had affected me.

At the end of July I returned to the first team at Grace Road, Leicester, then on to Canterbury where 19-year-old Colin Cowdrey scored 90 against the bowling of Shack, Vic, Gerry and Charlie Knott. Colin played the ball so late and with such perfect timing that my intuitive anticipation at cover point was nullified.

It was not until the fifth game of my reinstatement that I came into good form. As against the Gloucester spin twins in the previous season, my concentration moved into 'the zone' when batting against Appleyard and Wardle, Trueman and Leadbeater at Headingley in a long battle to try to save the match. Batting at number four I was eventually bowled by Appleyard for 64. The *Yorkshire Evening Post* gave me a good write-up, and the Yorkshire and England captain, Norman Yardley, came into our dressing room to congratulate and encourage me. A long-remembered moment!

After long hours on trains from Leeds to Southampton, a very late night and five hours' sleep I encountered the fastest bowling in my career thus far, from the young blond South African, Cuan McCarthy.

The super-quick McCarthy bowled 20 overs, taking two wickets for 18 runs, but Alan survived against him, scoring a calm 26. He also scored 26 in the second innings. His form was finally returning. Unfortunately, with three fixtures remaining, that marked the end of Alan's season.

Match over, hasty friendly farewells, transport waiting: South Africans to London, Hampshire to Birmingham, to be followed by matches against Essex and Sussex at Bournemouth. In that last match of Neil McCorkell's long career Desmond Eagar handed the coin to Mac to toss with fellow veteran Jim Langridge. Dear Mac had been a wonderful friend and mentor to me, and that event may have misted my eyes if I had been there.

But the day after saying farewell to the South Africans I donned my mothballed RAF uniform, caught a bus to the New Forest and reported for two weeks of duty at RAF Sopley, a radar communications unit and filter room. As a result of tensions with Russia, and British involvement in the Korean War, reservists were being called in for refresher courses and training on new equipment.

When the fortnight was over, I was relieved to be out of the itchy uniform and able again to enjoy Betty's companionship and cooking, music on the radio and playtime with Denis. Playtime, too, at Dean Park where Hampshire Past played Hampshire Present in serious-fun cricket to entertain a jovial crowd of spectators for George Heath's Benefit. It was a great privilege to be on the field of play with all those well-known players of the past, especially with Johnny Arnold who had recovered from his serious illness.

September heralded change: from summer to autumn, from playing to working. I was not returning to Warnford because Betty and I planned to hire a hall and advertise ballroom dancing classes for beginners on one or two weekday evenings.

I needed a daytime job in Southampton and quickly; I could not waste time answering advertisements and hoping for interviews. While on duty at RAF Sopley I remembered that I had had an interesting chat in the Members' Bar at Northlands Road with a man who had mentioned that he was a director of the Pirelli General Cable Company, a huge manufacturing complex along the Western Esplanade. In the second week of September I wrote and posted a letter to him, requesting an interview.

However, the next day I decided to dress smartly and go to the Pirelli Works. Maybe I could talk my way past the receptionists and secretaries to see the man face to face. And I did! He gave me a job because of my initiative – bloody cheek – and the next Monday I sat at a clerk's desk in the shipping department. On Friday I opened a wage packet containing just over four pounds cash, net after the usual deductions.

Meanwhile the dancing classes gathered momentum.

During the summer Betty had searched for a suitable hall where we could teach ballroom dancing to beginners. There were three full-time schools of ballroom dancing in central Southampton and

Shirley but none to the east of the River Itchen in the Bitterne area. So from mid-September we rented the old Catholic Church Hall in Bitterne's Commercial Street on Saturday evenings. We advertised in the *Southern Daily Echo*: private lessons from six o'clock, a Beginners Class at eight.

Denis had developed into a physically healthy toddler with a determined character and inquisitive mind. The relationship between our landlady and Betty had grown into a friendship and Mrs Hunt, together with her young daughters, enjoyed looking after Denis when we went to a social function or the cinema. Hearing that we were planning to start dancing classes, she offered to put Denis to bed and babysit on Saturday evenings so that Betty could join me at the Bitterne hall by eight o'clock.

The first two classes for beginners were attended by less than twenty young people – more girls than boys – but from the third week onwards attendance rose to forty or more, and bookings for private lessons soon filled my diary from six to eight o'clock.

Ballroom dancing as a social activity was thriving throughout the country: from dinner dances in posh hotels to the Saturday night 'hop' at the Drill Hall; from the annual company, university or corporate ball to the cricket or tennis club's fund-raiser at the village hall.

The young uninitiated boys and girls needed to be able to 'get round the floor' with enough confidence to do so partnered by a member of the opposite sex – for many young beginners the most embarrassing and nerve-wracking experience. To 'get round the floor' required a basic mastery of a simple sequence of dance steps: the quarter turns, lock step and natural spin turn in the quickstep and the natural and reverse turns plus the natural spin turn in the slow waltz.

Betty taught the boys, I taught the girls …. fine. Teaching both groups 'the ballroom hold' and asking-pleading-coaxing them to 'partner up' was often difficult and sometimes hilarious. It became evident that Betty and I were 'good at this', that we created an enjoyable social atmosphere combined with warm authority and humour. The evidence was in the class sizes and bookings for private lessons: as we had no phone, lessons were booked at the classes or by occasional letter.

At some point in November I started to book the hall from two o'clock, and on most Saturdays I was fully booked through to eight without a break for a meal – tea, sandwiches and chocolate had to suffice. Betty arranged with Mrs Hunt to leave home at six o'clock to take private lessons from seven.

I hear a question, dear reader: 'Why an hour to travel six miles?' Buses! From St James Road to the Civic Centre, change and wait, from the Civic Centre to Bitterne Church, then walk two hundred yards in all weathers to the Catholic Hall. Until a padlocked storage cupboard in the church hall became available in the New Year, I lugged our equipment on and off the buses: a Phillips electric record player about the size and weight of two modern desktop printers, a large hessian shopping bag for a dozen shellac 78 rpm records, two bottles of milk, sugar, leaf tea and awful Camp Coffee in a bottle, two tea towels, a desk diary and my dance shoes. However, in those days with no car, luggage and push chairs and buses and walking miles was a normal everyday chore.

In January 1952 we started Intermediate and Medal classes on Friday evenings. I also started a Square Dance class at the Palm Court Ballroom in the Stadium. The landlord was Charlie Knott's father; he used to spy on the number of pupils I had, aiming to raise the rent. When the cricket season commenced, Betty continued the classes at Bitterne until the end of June. A big 'thank you' to Mrs Hunt!

The combined income from the job with Pirelli and our dance classes amounted to more than my annual wage from Hampshire County Cricket Club as a non-capped player.

8

Connections

Meditating on a conversation in 1951

In a 1929 short story the Hungarian author Frigyes Karinthy explored the intriguing idea that each one of us can be connected to every other human on the planet by no more than six direct links. It is sometimes called The Six Handshakes Rule.

This was an idea that fascinated Alan and, though he did not demonstrate the rule, he left a chapter in which he wove together the unlikely links between six men: Neil McCorkell, Gerry Hill's father Ernest, Arthur Conan Doyle, the Millfield headmaster RJO Meyer, Alan's son Denis and Dr Ken McCall, the psychiatrist whom Alan consulted in the 1960s.

It is a whimsical chapter, a delightful mix of elements, and it begins in The Hutch at Northlands Road one wet afternoon in July 1951. Neil McCorkell was in the final weeks of a county career that had started back in 1932, playing in a Hampshire side captained by Lord Tennyson and including such legends of the county as Philip Mead, George Brown and Alex Kennedy, all men in their forties who had established themselves well before the First World War. McCorkell had toured India under Lord Tennyson in 1936/37 and had opened the batting against all the great pre-war quicks, but he was not one to talk much about it all.

> Mac was a mature and friendly family man who chatted amiably with colleagues, but he rarely addressed the room. That afternoon Jim Bailey, now a smartly besuited businessman, visited us in The Hutch, and he encouraged Mac to recount his memories of the games, characters and quirky events of his long career.

Jim Bailey was a natural raconteur, Gerry Hill could talk, and the three of them, Hampshire team-mates from 1932 to 1949, were soon in full flow. At one stage they got onto the subject of Micky Walford, the Sherborne schoolmaster who each year dropped into the Somerset team in his holidays and scored runs galore. Alan, twelfth man that wet afternoon, lapped up their conversation, recreating it for this book as he imagined it might have happened.

Gerry: "I'll always remember that match at Weston when Micky Walford scored a double ton – beautiful stroke-maker."

Mac: "Yes, very talented and confident – and he was so good at placing the ball between fielders on both sides of the wicket."

Jim: "But he had a solid defence, too, and on that good wicket he was hard to get out – and we didn't really, he just ran out of puff!"

Gerry: "I remember we were struggling to avoid an innings defeat until you two dug in and scored about 140 together – which got under the skin of their eccentric skipper Jack Meyer. Didn't he bowl you some lobs one over, Jim ?"

RJO Meyer

"Lobs?" exclaimed Jim, raising the tone of his cultured baritone voice and both arms in the air. "*LOBS?!* No, Gerry, he bowled Spedegue's Droppers. He sent the ball so high! Jack was nuts but also very bright. He'd read that Spedegue story written by your Dad's friend, Gerry … that Conan Doyle chap. Anyway, Jack Meyer became frustrated and put himself on to bowl. In his first spell he had bowled gentle medium-paced out-swing, but now he started bowling liquorish all-sorts – medium-slow seamers, off and leg spin, all quite accurately from a five-yard run-up. And he was a fidget, changing his field nearly every ball.

"He'd bowled two overs of his mixture to Mac and me; I pulled one for four and we pushed a few singles. Before starting his third over he stood by the stumps and looked at me. 'I'm ready, Jim,' he said. 'Are you?' 'No run-up?' I queried. 'No run-up.'

"'What's he up to?' I thought. I walked up the pitch, tapping down non-existent divots with the toe of my bat. I looked at you, Mac, and you shook your head. I returned to the popping crease and asked umpire Joe Hills for 'middle', and I scratched my guard in the dust with my boot studs.

"This delaying tactic riled Jack Meyer who was standing sideways beside the stumps, feet apart, both arms outstretched, ready to deliver. He then began to rock from left foot to right foot – about five times – swung his straight right arm down below his hips and up again – releasing the ball just above head level. Up and up she went – so high it was difficult to judge the trajectory – then down, down – I watched – it was going to land a few yards behind the keeper, Wally Luckes, who stepped back a few paces and caught it.

Next ball up up up, then coming down – maybe close to my wicket so I turned to face the stumps, ducked my head and bowed. The ball hit me on my bum. The third was going to land straight and on a full length so, watching the ball all the way down I stood astride the pitch, bat held high and facing the bowler ... *an' I trapped 'er with the face of me bat into the dry pitch.*"

This last bit was delivered with a broad rural Hampshire accent.

Mac spoke up: "Wally and the close-in fielders were laughing; Harold called out from mid-wicket, 'Yoom gotta a fine fat arse, Jim boy.' I was close to Jack Meyer who looked serious and commanded, 'Get me that ball, Wally.' Umpire Hills was also only a few feet from Jack Meyer; he had a hankie in his hand pretending to blow his nose to disguise his swallowed laughter. 'Let's get on with it,' ordered Meyer ... and up she went again, even higher."

Uproar in The Hutch – laughter, happy tears and a hubbub of questions to Jim, Mac and Gerry. I was doubled up from laughing when Leo Harrison's voice penetrated the din: "I was there. I saw it all, and Mad Jack's steeplers were ..." Then someone cut in: "Not cricket!"

When the questions and the banter had subsided, Jim told us that, when sharing a pint with some of the Somerset players after the game, Micky Walford had told him about Arthur Conan Doyle's story *Spedegue's Dropper*.

The Story of Spedegue's Dropper, published in the *Strand* magazine in 1928, told the tale of a young schoolmaster with a weak heart whose passion for cricket was not matched by any ability. In a clearing in the New Forest he and his brother fixed a rope to two trees, and with much practice he perfected the art of tossing a cricket ball high above the rope to land exactly 22 yards away. In no time he was a sensation, called up by England and winning a Test against Australia at Lord's.

A tall, thin young man was lobbing balls from one end.

Spedegue played no more cricket. His heart would not stand it. His doctor declared that this one match had been one too many and that he must stand out in the future. But for good or for bad — for bad, as many think — he has left his mark upon the game for ever. The English were more amused than exultant over their surprise victory. The Australian papers were at first inclined to be resentful, but then the absurdity that a man from the second eleven of an unknown club should win a Test Match began to soak into them, and finally Sydney and Melbourne had joined London in its appreciation of the greatest joke in the history of cricket.

Arthur Conan Doyle, a doctor by training, was a gifted sportsman. In the 1880s, while practising medicine in Southsea, he attended the inaugural meeting of Portsmouth Association Football Club, keeping goal for them for five years. He boxed, played golf and billiards to a good standard and appeared in cricket matches for many teams, including for MCC in ten first-class games.

By the standards of the day, his batting average of 19.25 was respectable, but he is remembered more for his one first-class wicket, that of WG Grace. In later life he honoured the moment with a 19-verse poem, three stanzas of which Alan included in this chapter:

> Once in my heyday of cricket –
> One day I shall ever recall! –
> I captured that glorious wicket,
> The greatest, the grandest of all.
>
> Before me he stands like a vision,
> Bearded and burly and brown,
> A smile of good humoured derision,
> As he waits for the first to come down.
>
> A statue from Thebes or Knossos,
> A Hercules shrouded in white,
> Assyrian bull-like colossus,
> He stands in his menacing might.

Late in his life Conan Doyle bought a second home, a writing retreat, in the New Forest – a secluded house, Bagnell Wood, in the village of Brook near Minstead. There he wrote *The Story of Spedegue's Dropper*, pursued his interest in spiritual matters and played golf at the Bramshaw course. It was during a round of golf in 1929 that he changed the course of a young man's life. Let Alan tell the story.

> Sir Arthur Conan Doyle had driven straight but short from the 18th tee and joined his golfing friend Ernest Hill to walk the fairway which ran alongside the local cricket ground. Arthur paused for a moment to watch the villagers playing a match, then turned to Ernest: "That young lad can play a bit," he said.
> "Ah, yes," smiled Ernest Hill. "That's my son Gerry. He's sixteen."
> Born in 1913, Gerald Hill was nurtured by his parents in the country environment of their smallholding in Brook, a hamlet adjacent to Bramshaw. In addition to working the smallholding Ernest was also the local postman; he probably met Sir Arthur when delivering bags of mail to Bignell Wood.
> Later that summer, while watching the young cricketer playing for Bramshaw, Arthur and Ernest discussed Gerry's career possibilities. Impressed by the young man's talent and quiet enthusiastic

personality, Sir Arthur wrote to the Secretary of Hampshire CCC, recommending him for a trial.

Records show that Gerry played for the Club & Ground XI in 1931 and made his first class debut for Hampshire the next year, aged 19. Jim Bailey and Neil McCorkell played in the match.

Alan and Betty had christened their first-born Denis Gerald Alan, with the Gerald inspired by the kindness of Gerry Hill.

> Gerry Hill, an upright character and family man, had been a friend and caring mentor to me in my first season. He was a countryman, a New Forester who was a good shot, ran with the hounds and in his youth rode a New Forest pony. A golf handicap of four became scratch when he played regularly. Denis enjoyed chatting with Gerry at Sunday charity matches in the late 1950s and early '60s, and I always enjoyed Gerry's company at social events and reunions. He died in 2006.

The connection with Denis leads back to the match at Weston-super-Mare and RJO Meyer's bowling of Spedegue droppers.

Jack Meyer was a freethinking pioneer, right up Alan's street. After graduating from Cambridge University he had become a cotton trader in India. There, playing cricket, he came into contact with Ranjitsinhji, who persuaded him to give up cotton trading and teach at his Princely School. In 1932, the 27-year-old Meyer moved on to become headmaster at a school owned by a Maharajah, who three years later persuaded Meyer to set up a school in England, to prepare his sons and those of other Indian royals for an English public school and university education.

Although Alan had seen Meyer on the cricket field when he captained Somerset at Lord's, he was first to meet him in his position as headmaster of the school he had created, Millfield in Street, Somerset, an establishment that had grown exponentially from its first small beginnings with the sons of Indian royalty.

> Denis attended Highfield Church School in Southampton and passed the 'eleven-plus' examination in 1961. He also captained the Southampton Schools Under-12 cricket team against Portsmouth Schools.
>
> As a a keen supporter of co-education I was unhappy that there were no co-ed grammar schools in Southampton west of the river Itchen. Denis went to King Edward's Grammar School for Boys

where the headmaster was an authoritarian egotist. He conducted his first parent interview with Betty and me sitting behind a desk on a raised dais wearing an academic gown and mortar board. I was fuming! I was determined to move our academically bright son to a more liberal, and preferably co-ed, school.

Due to career changes we were financially poor; we had four children and for two pounds a week were renting a not unpleasant semi-detached house in Portswood. The dining room was my office from which I was in the process of creating my own estate agency.

Early in 1962 I was inspired by an article in the *Sunday Times*, praising the bold enterprise of Jack Meyer as founder and headmaster of Millfield School in Somerset, now a leader in modern progressive education. I immediately wrote a long letter to Mr RJO Meyer, requesting consideration for a scholarship place for Denis, outlining his academic and sporting achievements. I also summarised my thoughts about King Edward's School and my reasons for retiring from county cricket and closing the ballroom dancing business.

The answer was positive. First there was a psychological test, which was successful, to be followed by an appointment with The Boss at Millfield in May. 'Bring his cricket gear,' the letter stated.

In our dumpy Ford Squire station wagon Denis and I headed west through Wiltshire into Somerset along a variety of A and B roads for about eighty miles, arrived early at Millfield School, unusual for me, and waited a long time outside The Boss's study – evidently usual.

Eventually the study door burst open. A swirling academic gown below busy eyes appeared, the voice emitting a stream of instructions to an invisible aide inside the room. I glimpsed piles of papers and books before being grasped around my shoulder and hearing the words, "Good to see a Hampshire cricketer, Alan. To the nets with your son!" as we were hastened through the main door to a gravelled courtyard.

Looking around, he called to the nearest boy: "Watkins, organise tea for three. We'll be by the oak tree in the lower field … thank you."

With Denis in our wake and Jack firing off question after question we crossed a boundary line at a trot, disturbed a house match, marched through the centre of the pitch – batsmen, bowlers and umpires motionless – beyond the far boundary to a garden table and chairs by a large oak tree. Phew!

"Pad up, Denis." Then to a nearby group of boys watching the match, The Boss called out, "We need two bowlers."

Before walking over to the net Jack asked me about my summer of coaching at Lord's in 1959, why I had not stayed there, and I quickly explained my reasons.

"I understand" said Jack. "What are your ambitions?"

"Too many," I replied. "The family is my priority."

I stood beside Jack as he supervised the bowlers and appraised the batting style and technique of my son.

"Pitch the balls up, boys: we need half volleys outside the off stump to see what his cover drive is like."

For his age Denis was a promising right-handed batsman – although inclined to be 'bottom handed'.

"Ah, too much right hand too early," confided Jack as he left my side to walk down the net, chat to Denis and demonstrate an off-drive with only his left hand high on the bat handle: "Hold on tight and follow right through with the left hand. Your right hand needs a lighter grip; the thumb, index and middle finger of your right hand will provide the power on impact."

Denis had a strong stubborn streak in his nature and was inclined to resist instructions in the immediate moment and respond, one way or another, after thinking about 'it'. No time to think on this occasion because moments later one of the bowlers pitched a ripe half volley outside the off-stump, and Denis played a classic and beautiful cover drive. The picture has remained in my mind-video library to this day!

The Boss clapped and called out, "That's it. Wonderful cover drive, young Rayment." Then he turned to me and said, "I'll take him – arrange a scholarship – would five pounds a term be alright, Alan? You pay for books and laundry, of course. And if your new business is a success you could pay more – say, fifty pounds per term."

I was stunned and momentarily speechless. At that time the full boarding fees were over a thousand pounds a year.

"Thank you, Mr Meyer, I'm more than grateful. I'm sure that Denis will be very pleased."

Denis had passed his bat and pads to one of the bowling boys and was himself trundling leg-breaks and having fun. I called him over and shared the news. Denis thanked The Boss and even called him Sir!

As the great Somerset batsman Harold Gimblett used to say, "Jack could charm the hairs from a gooseberry."

Tea and cakes had arrived. I poured, Jack talked. I have forgotten the detail, but I remember his theme was education. He was passionate about bringing to light the unexplored talent within young people, male and female, by creating opportunity for development through art and music, through sport and athletics, science, nature and practical crafts as well as a high standard of academic study and achievement.

An enthusiast, a pioneer! I was very impressed!

Alan sold his estate agency business in 1965, moving the family to Lymington to enable their second son, Martin, to attend an excellent co-ed grammar school at Brockenhurst.

I was an active Christian and an inactive businessman working in temporary jobs – selling cars and cleaning windows – for low wages. Although family life was buoyant and the five children energetic and resourceful, the birth of Peter in June 1966 increased the strain on our finances and marital relationship. I experienced a moderate level of anxiety and depression. Our GP, Dr Ralph Leach, who had been a Christian missionary in Ruanda, referred me to his friend, psychiatrist Dr Kenneth McAll who lived in Bignell Wood, Conan Doyle's old house in Brook.

Born in China to missionary parents Kenneth McAll attended medical school at Edinburgh University and returned to China with his wife in the mid-1930s during the second Sino-Japanese war. As medical missionaries they were in great demand but also often in great danger from advancing Japanese soldiers or fanatical guerrilla groups. In the war he and his wife were interned by the Japanese and suffered harrowing times as prisoners of war. Their experiences of guidance and protection, of answered prayers for healing and exorcism, raised their levels of faith from believing to 'knowing'.

In his autobiography he wrote that, when they returned to England after the war, they were 'weary in mind and body and weighing little more than six stone'. For seven years they were partners in a rural general practice but Doctor Ken was *'troubled by the many inexplicable things I had seen and heard in China that could not be brushed aside.'*

In 1956 he returned to university to specialise in psychiatry, to live and work in English mental hospitals and learn all he could about mentally disturbed and violent people. In the early 1960s he purchased the Tudor-style house, Bignell Wood, which was reputed by the villagers of Brook to be haunted.

My seven visits to Bignell Wood are etched in my memory. On the second visit Doctor Ken shared with me some of the *unexpected happenings* he and his wife and children experienced soon after they moved into the property. The four younger children, a nurse and a visitor had all seen 'the tall old man with a moustache' or heard sliding doors to cupboards being opened at night.

Doctor Ken told me that he knew the 'unsettled spirit' was that of Conan Doyle who was looking for a diary that he wished to be burned in the garden. The local vicar said that several villagers had been scared by an apparition which their car headlights lit up on dark nights – they knew 'it' was Conan Doyle. Prayers were held at the house to heal and free the 'unsettled spirit', and there were no more manifestations of the former resident.

Ken McCall was a psychic and a spiritual healer as well as a medical scientist. He was the first person to *really understand* the life-changing spiritual encounters I experienced in 1957 and 1958 – which was such a relief. He became a friend who supported and advised me, often by means of long-distance telephone conversations, through major life changes during the next eighteen years of my life. No medications: deep insights, talking therapy and common sense. Thank you, Ken McAll!

And so Alan's chapter ended, a long way from The Hutch where the old cricketers reminisced happily about bygone days.

I raise a symbolic glass in praise of Jim Bailey, the all-round Hampshire cricketer and raconteur who told the tale that led me 69 years after that memorable afternoon to join these experiences and people together.

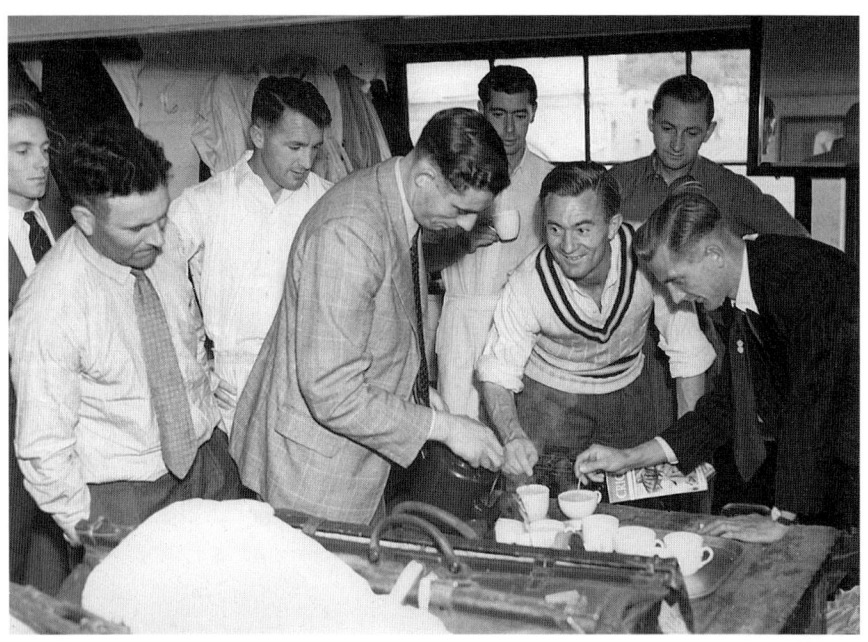

Tea time in 1951: (from left) Alan Rayment, Gerry Hill, Neville Rogers, Reg Dare, Derek Shackleton, Vic Cannings, Cliff Walker, Leo Harrison

Cards in 1952: (standing) Rayment, Gray, Hill, Rogers, Walker, Carty, Holt; (sitting) Dare, Prouton, Shackleton, Cannings, Harrison

Cards in 1954: Derek Shackleton and Leo Harrison, watched by Reg Dare, Alan Rayment, Ralph Prouton, Arthur Holt, Don Cartridge and Mervyn Burden

1955: Harry Altham, Desmond Eagar, Roy Marshall, Derek Shackleton, Alan Rayment, Ray Pitman and Dick Carty (with Alan's reflection in the mirror)

9

Four summers of county cricket
1952 – 1955

Alan studied the statistics of his Hampshire cricket for this book, and he could not shake off a feeling that he had not scored the runs he should have done. Across ten summers, from 1949 to 1958, in 198 matches for the county, he scored 6,333 runs, with four centuries and 23 fifties, at an average of 20.36.

Combined with his outstanding fielding and his cheerful spirit, he did enough with the bat to remain in the side as a regular, or near-regular, from the start of 1952 to the middle of 1957 – but, even in an era of damp summers and uncovered pitches, there were too many low scores between the occasional triumphs, and he knew it.

Wisden wrote one year that he 'could be a delightful batsman to watch but he suffered unaccountable lapses of concentration.' It is an easy charge to make against any batsman who looks to play his shots, but in Alan's case there was probably some truth in it. His approach to life was never quite compatible with the workaday application expected of a professional. He played some memorable defensive knocks when the team was in trouble, but at other times he would fall to an over-ambitious shot.

Perhaps he was too much of an amateur in spirit, without quite the ability to succeed consistently with a carefree approach. That is the implication behind his own explanation for his moderate record.

> I scored nowhere near enough runs for the talent I had, partly because I enjoyed it too much, partly because – as I look at it now – after I'd been awarded my cap I thought I had achieved what I set out to do. If we were not in trouble, I was too cavalier.

Hampshire were in trouble against Somerset at Portsmouth in May 1952. With rain having ruined their first fixture at Edgbaston, Alan was batting for the first time in the summer – and, with his contract running out at the end of the year, he knew that he needed to grasp the opportunity presented by Neil McCorkell's retirement.

Cliff Walker and Jimmy Gray had been dismissed cheaply, and Leo Harrison had limped off, having ricked his back after pulling a ball for four. It was 26 for two, effectively 26 for three, when Alan went to the wicket, and soon enough another three wickets fell.

With support from the lower order – Gerry Hill, Derek Shackleton and Reg Dare – Alan kept his head down. When last-man Vic Cannings came to the wicket, he was still there, on 83.

Alan (left) and Vic Cannings come out after tea

Vic did his best to stay long enough to get Alan to his maiden century, but off the fourth ball of an over from the fast but erratic Maurice Tremlett he was bowled, leaving Alan tantasingly short on 95 not out. It was his highest first-class score, beating his 94 at Bournemouth in the last game of 1950, but it was not a century.

Just as they were starting to leave the field, there was a signal from Desmond Eagar – "Stay out there" – and a badly limping Leo Harrison emerged, accompanied by a runner. Amid excitement Harrison survived the last two balls of the over, then he came down the wicket to speak to Alan.

> He said to me, "Hurry up and hit the runs, Al. I want to put my leg up again."

Alan duly hit a four off Bertie Buse, ran a single and came off with 100 not out. His maiden century had been scored in four hours and 10 minutes. 'It sounds slow,' Joe Hulme wrote in *The People*. 'But it didn't look slow. And as a rescue act it was grand stuff.' Another Sunday paper called it 'a dogged knock, enlivened by delightful drives and ten fours'.

In a match in which no other batsman on either side reached 40 and the great Harold Gimblett was out for a pair, Alan hit a confident 74 in his second innings. 'His play on the off-side was particularly pleasing to watch,' reported the *Southern Daily Echo*.

John Arlott remained a great admirer, writing that 'his confidence is drawing level with his powers':

> With one of the most attractive techniques one could wish to see, he lights up the long-neglected off-side with strokes in the grand manner. He has a quick brain, equally quick feet and a polish in execution which is completely characteristic of him. He is calm and he is modest ... He is almost incapable of playing a dull innings. He will treat good bowling with respect, but his style is such that he is always good to watch for those with a genuine eye for cricket.

His batting even occasioned an article in *The Dancing Times* under the headline 'THIS BOY ALWAYS DRAWS A CROWD':

> And you're wrong! It's not Frank Sinatra, but Hampshire professional cricketer Alan Rayment, who runs a studio in Bitterne, Southampton.
>
> Footnote: Alan has a two-way recipe – For good dancing, play cricket; for good cricket, practise dancing!

Another article on the same theme was headlined 'He's Got Dancing Feet'.

> The 25-year-old Hampshire batsman brings the steps of a dancing master into his free-scoring batting.

A second century followed in early June, against Nottinghamshire at Trent Bridge. Then, at Bournemouth in late July, after he had top-scored with a resolute 48 against Glamorgan, Alan achieved his dream in what he called 'a properly proud moment'. On the field, before the start of the next day's play, Desmond Eagar presented him with his county cap. He had established himself at last, and his weekly wage, paid all year round, rose from five pounds to seven pounds and 15 shillings.

Did the cap affect Alan, as he suggested? It is an unanswerable question, but his scores in the last weeks of that summer do support the theory. By the first week of August he had hit 927 runs, only 73 short of the special milestone of 1,000. Yet four weeks later, having played ten more innings, he went to the middle for the last time still short of the 1,000. Happily he ended the season in style, his 58 against the touring Indians rescuing the county and setting up a thrilling run chase in which the Indians, needing 106 for victory, finished on 100 for eight.

In the previous winter, when Alan's future in cricket had looked uncertain, he and Betty had hatched a plan to move to Australia. The country, keen to build up its population, was offering a £10 passage to Britons wanting to settle there.

> Betty and I were very independent. If we wanted to do something, we just did it. We filled in the forms, and we got quite excited about it. But I had another year's contract and, when I won my county cap, our thinking changed.

Staying in Southampton, they arranged to have a house built in Lordswood Gardens, next to the sports centre, and they opened a dance studio at the Hamtum House Hotel in Hulse Road. In the hotel garden was an orchard with a wall, on the other side of which was the County Ground.

*

Alan's notes on the next summer, 1953, do not make happy reading.

> 28 matches, 48 innings, one century, four innings over 40, 19 innings under 20 **and** 7 ducks (including a pair). Average 20.09. Comment today – pathetic! Even on wet uncovered wickets. I am angry with myself because I had a lot of talent. Though still madly enthusiastic, I was probably not serious enough ... still half-amateur, half-professional. Betty and Den and I *should* (one of my hate words) have emigrated to Australia.
>
> After the season we bought our first car – from a gipsy car sales field at West End. Paid £70 for a Standard Flying 20 1937.
>
> From cricket I earned £450, including win and talent money.

Alan's summer started with a pre-season friendly against an Isle of Wight side, to mark the opening of a new sports ground at Cowes. He scored a confident 35, batting with the white West Indian Roy Marshall, who had given up his faltering Test career and was starting two years of qualification for Hampshire. At Cowes his innings of 56 impressed the local reporter.

> Marshall was in holiday mood from the start. Batting with that deceptively leisurely style which gives spectators the impression that he is scoring boundaries, merely to save the trouble of running, he set the pace at a rate of 100 runs an hour.

The disinclination to run quick singles was one that Jimmy Gray would discover when he became Marshall's opening partner. "Even when I played squash with Roy, he wasn't keen on too much movement; he just stood there with those rapier wrists and made me do all the running. And if you batted with him, you were never sprinting ones. He went on a Cavaliers tour to Jamaica with Peter Richardson. Peter was all application and push and, with Roy at the other end, he couldn't get any runs. So they got into an argument. 'I'm not rushing up and down with you,' Roy said. 'You want to learn to hit the ball.'"

Not able to play in championship matches, Marshall hit 81 in a two-day friendly against Somerset, followed by 122 against The Army in the game in which Henry Horton arrived from Southampton Football Club, made 99 and was promptly added to the Hampshire batting line-up.

Alan's progress hit a new peak at Bristol on Saturday 30 May when he made 126, the highest score of his career, putting on 246 for the fourth wicket with Cliff Walker. With the Coronation on Tuesday, they played two long days so that they could start after lunch on the third. The Hampshire team watched the ceremony on a small television installed in their dressing room.

A week later the Australians, ahead of the first Test, came to Southampton, a match which attracted a crowd of 15,000 to the ground. Winning the toss, the visitors opted to bat.

> I was fielding at cover point. When the first ball from Shack landed, it created a mini-explosion of dust. The groundsman used to put lime on the best wickets, and the lime had rotted the grass roots. Desmond Eagar came rushing up. "Oh shit," he said. "That's the third day's gate gone." Then on that spitting wicket Neil Harvey scored an amazing hundred.

Despite Harvey's runs Eagar was proved right, the match ending on the second day with Hampshire bowled out for 131 and 148. Roy Marshall hit a 'sparkling' 71 in the second innings, and the next highest score by a Hampshire batsman was 30 by Alan.

> I hit a six off Richie Benaud that cleared the wall and landed in the orchard of the Hamtum Hill Hotel.

Hampshire versus the Australians at Southampton, June 1953
Neil Harvey batting, Alan covering a wide area in the covers

Little else survives of Alan's memories of the summer. Bizarrely the website CricketArchive and the Hampshire yearbook (not published till 1999) both record him as captaining the side at Northampton in the absence of Desmond Eagar, when it was Gerry Hill. "They must have looked at my three initials and thought I was an amateur," he used to joke.

In the last game, against Surrey at Bournemouth, he needed a pair of fifties to get him to the coveted 1,000 runs, but he was out for just 1 and 7, caught and bowled both times by Tony Lock.

> I remember hitting the ball hard and flat, about twelve inches off the turf, bisecting the wicket and mid-off. Four, I thought straightaway. Then a hand, followed by a telescopic arm, entered my sight line, followed by a balding head, wisps of ginger hair and a horizontal body. It was as if the hand was magnetised to the ball. When I came back in, Shack said to me, "Ee, that's tough, Al. Locky'd dive under a bus for a caught and bowled."

*

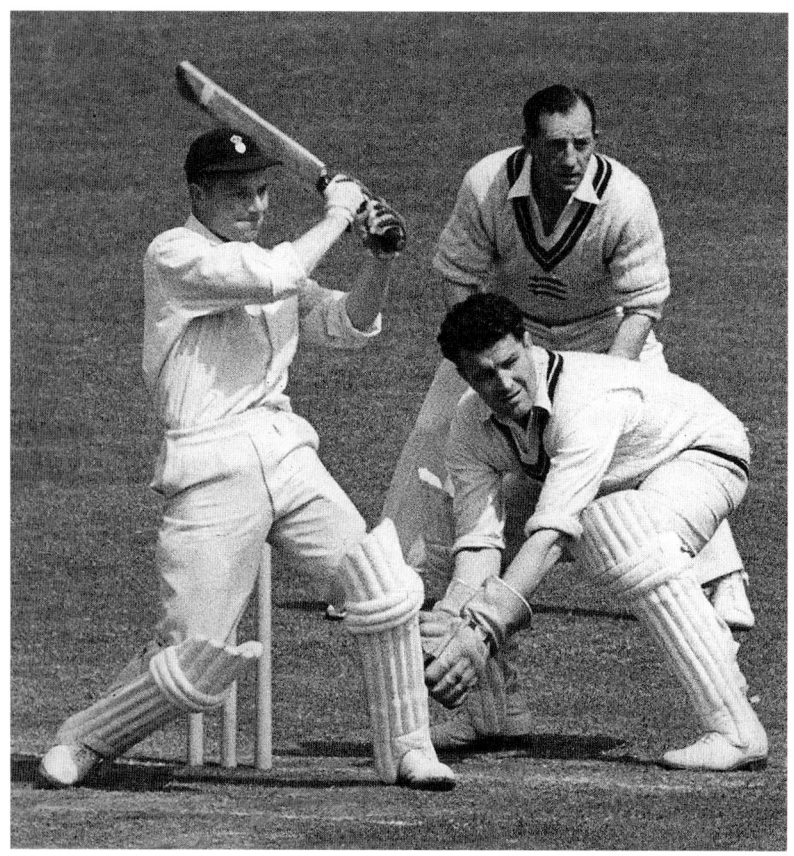

*Pulling his hero Denis Compton for four at Lord's in May 1954
Bill Edrich at slip, Leslie Compton keeping wicket*

The summer of 1954 was the coldest and gloomiest of the 20th century, and in these conditions Alan's cricket did not prosper. He started well, top-scoring in each innings at Lord's with 40 and 65, but he failed to score another fifty all summer, spending six weeks out of the team in mid-season.

> While fielding at third man at Portsmouth against Leicestershire I had a minor mystical experience, a type of meditative dialogue with 'someone' outside of self, debating "How much longer am I going to play cricket for a living? There are a lot of things to do in life ..."

The next summer, 1955, was a much warmer one, but for Alan it looked like following the same course as the summer of 1954. In the first game against Glamorgan he top-scored with a crucial 48 not out. Then there followed a run of low scores, leading to his losing his place in the team in early July.

During away matches some of the Hampshire team did not venture far from the ground and the hotel, but Alan had a curiosity that often led him to explore the towns and cities where they were playing. At Bradford, he recalled, he and Jimmy Gray spent an evening in working men's pubs, observing the very different way of life of the northern city.

Although Alan was out for a duck, lbw to Ray Illingworth, the Bradford game brought Hampshire their first victory on Yorkshire soil since 1932 – and by an innings. Yorkshire, batting on a sticky wicket, were all out twice in a day, with Peter Sainsbury on his 21st birthday dismissing Len Hutton cheaply in both innings.

Hutton had captained England to victory in Australia the previous winter, but a combination of exhaustion, both mental and physical, and persistent rheumatism led to his standing down from Test cricket for the summer. His form for Yorkshire was poor, but a fortnight later at Trent Bridge he was back to his best, hitting 194, with the last 94 coming in little more than an hour. The hope among English cricket lovers was that he was now fully recovered and would be his old self for the arrival of the Australians in 1956.

From Trent Bridge Hutton travelled down to Bournemouth where, put in to bat on a tricky wicket, he faced the first ball. Derek Shackleton opened the bowling, and in his second over, without a run on the board, Hutton looked to play to leg a ball which lifted spitefully, caught the outside of his bat and spooned into the off-side where Alan, running back, took a good catch over his shoulders.

> When he passed me, returning to the pavilion, he looked pale and exhausted.

Unknown to Alan or anybody else watching that day, Hutton had woken in such pain that he had needed an osteopath to get him to the ground. In the second innings, batting down the order, he spent, in the words of the *Yorkshire Post*, '20 rather uneasy minutes over two singles before he slashed indiscreetly at Marshall outside the off stump and was caught at the wicket.' He returned home to Leeds, knowing that he had played for the last time.

From Bournemouth the Hampshire team travelled along the coast to Eastbourne for the game of the season – though foremost in Alan's memory was the banquet they attended on the second evening. From the top table the mayor of Eastbourne announced to them all that Alan was now the father of a baby girl, born that day – his third child and first daughter, Val.

Alan and Betty, with Martin, Denis and Valerie

I was not allowed to visit Betty and Val because there was a bug in the hospital. We met at a wire-fence boundary, with Betty in a dressing gown.

In a low-scoring encounter Hampshire were left to score 140 on the final day, and they looked in control at 55 for two as lunch approached. Henry Horton had 19, Alan 30, and the fielders, who earlier had been clustered round the bat, were starting to retreat. Then two lbws changed the course of the contest: Horton 'playing a rather careless head-in-the-air shot' to the off-spinner Robin Marlar, Alan 'beaten all ends up' by the slow left-armer Don Smith.

Alan's innings of 31 and 30 made him the top scorer on either side, but his runs looked in vain when Hampshire slid to 84 for eight. With 56 still wanted, all that stood between Sussex and victory was the young Peter Sainsbury and the tailenders Vic Cannings and Mervyn Burden.

It was a story that Vic Cannings always enjoyed telling:

> Robin Marlar was the Sussex captain. At Eastbourne there's a big tower with a clock that rings out every quarter, and I'd just got off the mark with a single when the clock boomed. I was big-headed now because I'd got off the mark, and I said to Robin who was at gully, "You'll hear that bloody thing a few times before I'm gone."

> We went on. Got some more runs. I was batting with Peter Sainsbury. Peter snicked one through Alan Oakman's legs at slip for four, and that brought us level. One to win. Then he got out last ball of the over, and Mervyn Burden came in. They said he had a pile of fags where he'd been smoking.
>
> I had it all worked out. Thomson was bowling, and Webb the keeper was standing back. I said to Mervyn, "I'm going to go down the wicket, let the ball hit me and keep running." But I missed the bloody ball, and it bowled me.

A week later Alan lost his place in the side, only returning in mid-August after a wrenched knee put Desmond Eagar out of action for the season.

In his first match back, in a low-scoring game against Lancashire at Portsmouth, Alan's 31 and 27 made him – as against Sussex – the top scorer on either side, crucial runs in a narrow victory. Then a week later, against Somerset at Weston-super-Mare, he played the innings of his life.

There was rain before play on the Wednesday, but batting was not too difficult at first. Roy Marshall fell early, but Jimmy Gray and Henry Horton took the score to 78 without alarm. Then more rain fell, the spinners got to work on the increasingly sticky surface, and Hampshire were all out for 154.

> The pitch was wicked. All the time you were batting, you had to keep patting it down with the back of your bat. There was a rumour that they had had a fair or a circus on it.

Roy Marshall was appalled by its state:

> I had never seen anything like it in my life. How people expected cricket to be played properly in these conditions is beyond me.

Seven days earlier, also at Weston, Somerset had been bowled out by Surrey for 36, the lowest score of the summer, and they looked unlikely to pass that when they collapsed to 10 for five. It was only thanks to wicket-keeper Harold Stephenson, who hit a few blows off Peter Sainsbury, that they got to 39.

Sainsbury took one wicket, there was a run out, and the other eight batsmen all fell to Derek Shackleton, whose final figures were 11.1 overs, 7 maidens, 8 wickets for 4 runs. There was a substantial prize for the best bowling figures of the season, and the previous day Worcestershire's Jack Flavell had laid claim to it by taking 9/30 at Dover. The story goes that when the ninth wicket fell to a run out by Sainsbury, Shack was not best pleased. "Eee, Sains," he grumbled, "you've just done me out of 100 guineas."

In mid-morning on the second day, when Alan stepped out to bat, the Hampshire score was 16 for two. On this most wretched of pitches, the last 16 wickets had fallen for 58 runs.

> Batting was almost impossible on that wicket so I decided to go crazy. Shit or bust. Jump up the wicket – dance, dance, dance – and go crash, bang, wallop. Jack McMahon, their Australian, was bowling, and I got him so mad that he lost his length.
>
> It was a miserable day, and I don't think there was much of a crowd. After a time there was some mild clapping. Leo Harrison, who was batting with me, came up and said, "Well done, Al." I didn't know what he meant. He said, "You've got a hundred." I had no idea. I was in a reverie, just thinking to myself 'This is fun'.
>
> Boldness does sometimes bring luck. I was, and still am, amazed that I reached 104. Dear Henry Horton and Leo Harrison survived to help me, and we declared on 245 for seven.

On the same surface on which Derek Shackleton had taken eight wickets for four runs, McMahon's three wickets cost 122. Then Somerset slumped to 16 for five. Again Stephenson attacked Sainsbury, hitting a quick 52, and Somerset were all out for 98.

The headlines all went to Derek Shackleton, whose six for 25 in 16 overs gave him the remarkable match figures of 14 for 29 in 27.1 overs, the joint cheapest 14-wicket tally in the long history of first-class cricket. Yet, in the context of the match, Alan's century was almost as remarkable.

It was Hampshire's 14th championship victory of the season, equalling their previous best in 1921, and they sat in third place in the table. Perennial also-rans, they had never finished higher than the fifth place they achieved in 1914 – so there was a buzz of excitement when they headed to Bournemouth for their last two matches. With Desmond Eagar out of action, they were captained by Neville Rogers in his last games before retirement.

Their opponents in the first match were Surrey, who the previous day had been crowned champions for the fourth successive year. And what a final day the match provided for the large crowd of holiday-makers and Hampshire supporters. *The Times* reckoned that it was 'the best crowd ever to watch a championship match in the county'.

In the morning, looking to set up a run chase for Surrey, the Hampshire batsmen – after a slow start – scored briskly, none more so than Neville Rogers and Alan. According to *The Times*, the pair 'added 66 in 35 minutes with an array of delightful strokes. They ran extremely well between the wickets, too, and Surrey even began to look ragged in the field.' Alan, 'who is surely capable of more runs than he makes', fell for 43, and at lunch Neville Rogers declared, leaving Surrey to make 304 in four hours. With a fast outfield and plenty of batting, the contest was well poised.

Surrey made a good start, putting on 56 for the first wicket. Then Neville Rogers 'throwing as he pivoted, hit the bowler's stumps with Stewart well out, and thereafter Hampshire moved forward with growing momentum.' As the sun dropped after tea, wickets fell and Surrey's hopes faded. Peter Sainsbury needed five wickets to reach 100 in his first full season, and there was a great roar of joy as he took his fifth – and the team's tenth – when the Surrey captain Stuart Surridge 'was stumped, having strayed almost into Dorset.'

What scenes of celebration followed! Harry Altham, the county's President, spoke to the cheering crowd in front of the pavilion, calling it 'a great day for Hampshire cricket'. It was, as *The Times* made clear, 'their best season since their formation in 1863', and victory in the final game against Worcestershire ensured third place – behind Surrey and Yorkshire, both of whom they had beaten.

Alan had not had a productive season with the bat – 719 runs at an average of 19.97 – but he had found form in that heady last fortnight, scoring 237 runs in the final three championship matches, and he was the happy recipient of a pair of silver-and-enamel cuff-links which Desmond Eagar presented to each of the capped players.

With the exception of one appearance by the young Colin Ingleby-Mackenzie, standing in as keeper when Leo Harrison represented the Players against the Gentlemen at Lord's, Hampshire's championship campaign drew on only 13 players, and for the first time during Alan's years with the county their average age dipped below 30.

It had been the vision of Desmond Eagar to build a new team, youthful and dynamic in the field, and, with the astute support of coach Arthur Holt, the vision was now becoming a reality. Jimmy Gray, Mike Barnard, Peter Sainsbury, Mervyn Burden and Malcolm Heath, all local lads, promised much for the future, and the introduction of the 25-year-old Roy Marshall brought an attacking dash to the top-order batting. Despite the shock of the six-day schedule, with its long journeys between matches, Marshall far exceeded his captain's target for his first summer – 1,200 runs if he did some bowling, 1,500 if not – by taking 28 cheap wickets and topping 2,000 runs.

These were happy times for Hampshire, and Alan was an integral part of it.

10

Living life to the full
A successful dancing business

Alan and Betty's dance classes went from strength to strength. In the spring of 1954 they attended lessons in London's West End, where their teacher was Henry Jacques, three times British Professional Ballroom Champion in the 1930s and the author of the definitive instructional book 'Modern Ballroom Dancing'. Shortly afterwards Jacques emigrated with his dance partner to Australia, coming down to Southampton to buy Alan's old Standard 20 car so that he could shift all his belongings ahead of the move.

The lessons with Henry Jacques raised the level of their dancing and, in the winter of 1954/55, Alan and Betty won a heat of the International Ballroom Dancing Championship at Portsmouth, progressing to the final at the Royal Albert Hall, where they finished in a respectable 32nd place.

> We were in great demand all over the county, doing exhibitions and cabaret spots at dinner dances. I would wear tails, Betty a big dress, and we would perform the waltz, foxtrot, tango and quickstep, with the Viennese waltz for an encore. At somewhere like the Guildhall in Southampton, where there was a big floor, we could really motor.

Meanwhile the dance classes grew in popularity.

> There were a lot of dinner-dances in those days, and people wanted to be able to get round the floor at these functions. Also some of them were looking to meet a partner. We would run classes for thirty people, but we also had one-to-one private lessons, either for business people or for dancers who wanted to gain the Bronze, Silver and Gold medals.

Few of his fellow cricketers showed much interest, though he did persuade Malcolm Heath, Mike Barnard and Peter Sainsbury to come to a beginner's class at the Hamtum Hill Hotel.

> Pete was the only one who stuck with it. We prepared him for the Bronze medal, to be examined by Gwen Silvester, one of the legends of ballroom dancing, sister of Victor. Pete passed me in the passage

A ballroom dance exhibition by Betty and Alan

as he was going into the exam with Betty, and I saw with horror that his jaws were moving. I said, "Pete, you're not chewing gum in front of Gwen Silvester." He wouldn't go on to his Silver. He would have had to do the tango, and he said it was a 'silly' dance. What he meant was that it was too sexy!

In winter Alan was teaching full-time; in summer he gave it as much time as he could, slipping away at close of play whenever they were playing on the adjoining County Ground.

> There was just one bath in The Hutch, which everybody used, so I would have a wash-down with water from a basin, get dressed, have a quick half pint with the visitors and nip round to the hotel.
>
> One day Desmond said he wanted to see me in his office. "I hear you're taking private dance lessons after play," he said. "You can't go on doing this during the season. Cricket is your main occupation." It was done in a good spirit. He wasn't being a hard boss, he was just being Desmond. I said to him, "If you'll pay me what I earn at the dancing school, I will gladly stop."
>
> After that I did stay a little longer at the ground. I liked the social chat, but I was never a drinker.

The fee for a half-hour private class was 7/6; for a two-hour group, there were 30 people each paying 2/6. Yes, there were overheads but, with Betty also teaching and with bookings for exhibition dances, their income was far greater than the £450 a year that Hampshire were paying Alan – and it would rise significantly when they moved to larger premises.

> We were earning a lot of money, but it wasn't the money that motivated me. It was the fact that we were living very fully.

In the summer of 1955, when Betty was pregnant, student teachers ran many of the classes, and the demand continued to grow. Back in 1949, when Alan had started at Hampshire, his fellow newcomer Cliff Walker, whose family ran a chain of cinemas, had raised eyebrows among the professionals by arriving in a 1.5-litre Jaguar. Now, seven years on, it was Alan who had one, driving it at high speed to and from away games.

While Derek Shackleton had a reputation for driving with excessive care, never exceeding 45 miles an hour, Alan was the one none of them wanted to go with, just as Colin Ingleby-Mackenzie would soon become.

Malcolm Heath was the only one who would go with either of them. He told me about a journey with Ingleby-Mackenzie that I put in my first book.

> I've never driven with anyone quite like Colin when he was in form. "Dreadful machine, Malcolm, dreadful machine," he'd say. "I've got to get something faster than this." And the telegraph poles would go vroom, vroom, vroom. We used to go through a place called East Ilsley, up this long hill, and there always seemed to be a lorry ahead of us. There was a petrol station halfway up. One time we got up behind this lorry as fast as we could, then went round and through the petrol station and just came out in front of the lorry.

"That wasn't Colin," Alan protested when he read the book. "I was the one who did that. There was gravel and earth flying everywhere."

Early in 1956 Alan and Betty purchased a vacant site between The Dell and The Stadium, applying to build a large dance studio, with accommodation above. Planning permission was refused so, instead, they took over the run-down ballroom in Grosvenor Square, finalising the legal formalities only ten days before their advertised 'Grand Opening Dance' on Saturday 6 October.

They had enough money to hire a contractor to build a new foyer and gents toilet and to buy the required materials, but not for the labour, so Betty came up with the idea that they appeal to all their students to do the work. They arrived in droves, completing all the stripping out in three days, then setting to work on building and wiring up a low-level stage, creating a bar and a coffee bar decorated with bamboo, constructing and painting a false ceiling out of trellis, all this and much more, all in ten days.

What a triumph of community work it was! In 1967, at the age of 39, Alan enrolled at Birmingham University's Westhill College for a two-year, full-time course to obtain a Certificate in Community Work, a relatively new field of academic study. One of his first assignments was to write an essay about a personal experience that threw light on social attitudes to community, and he chose the ten-day conversion of the Grosvenor Ballroom.

> The day of the opening ball arrived, and still a lot had to be done. Being a Saturday there were plenty of helpers, but when the band arrived at 7pm for a 7.30 start they honestly believed they had come a week early – there was so much timber, sawdust, wire and wallpaper littering the floor. However, they entered into the spirit, took off their dinner jackets and helped to sweep out the rubbish. On the stroke of 7.30 they struck up their opening number, and on went the dance.

It was 'Southampton's gayest ballroom', and each Saturday night it was filled with 350 dancers.

ALAN and BETTY RAYMENT
HAVE PLEASURE IN ANNOUNCING THE OPENING TO THE PUBLIC OF THE

GROSVENOR BALLROOM

(Grosvenor Square, Southampton)

GRAND OPENING DANCE

SATURDAY, OCTOBER 6
(7.30—11.45 p.m.   4/-).
KENNY CLARKE'S MUSIC.

Your chance to win a FREE YEAR'S DANCING

Phone 20699

The GROSVENOR BALLROOM has been completely re-fitted and redecorated in contemporary style to make it Southampton's gayest ballroom. We have added a new foyer and fitted the refreshment room with a Bamboo Bar and will serve Gaggia Expresso Coffee for the first time.

We offer to the public a complete Ballroom Service— **Twice Weekly Dances, Ballroom Dancing Classes and Private Lessons in Ballroom, Latin American and Jive.**

DEMONSTRATIONS BY THE PRINCIPALS.

The Grosvenor Ballroom will be available for Hire for Private Functions on Thursdays.

PROGRAMME:

DANCING every Saturday and Wednesday, 7.30 p.m., to Kenny Clarke's Music.

BALLROOM CLASSES:
  MONDAYS: New Absolute Beginners' Class, 8—10 p.m. 2/6.
  TUESDAYS: Medal Class, 7.30—8.30. 2/-. Beginners' and Intermediate, 8.30—10.30. 2/6.

TEENAGERS' NIGHT:
  FRIDAY: Tuition, 7.30—8.0 p.m. 6d. Practice Dance, 8—10 p.m. 2/6.

Under 14's Class—SATURDAY, 3—4 p.m. 1/6.

PRIVATE LESSONS, BY APPOINTMENT, FROM 10 a.m. DAILY.

DON'T MISS THE OPENING NIGHT.—Tickets available at Grosvenor Ballroom, and at door.

Scenes from the opening night at the Grosvenor Ballroom: (top) Hampshire cricketers, Southampton footballers and their partners, (bottom) the band

Meanwhile their dance exhibitions continued to be in great demand.

For engagements at local venues we left staff in charge at about 9.30, changed into costume at the venue and performed sometime after 10 o'clock – always in a tearing rush, sometimes late. We left much earlier for out-of-town engagements in Bournemouth, Portsmouth, Winchester, Romsey, Lyndhurst, Ringwood, Barton-on-Sea and a few memorable village halls: one where nail heads protruded from the boards and another where I had to stop the band twice and ask them to play at half tempo. "Please, this is a dance, not a race."

Dancing on the beautiful floor of the Royal York Hotel in Ryde, Isle of Wight is particularly memorable, as is a performance on the Solent, on the sloping dance floor of the splendid 35,000-ton cruise ship RMS Caronia. Though secured to the quay at the Cunard terminal in Southampton Docks, the great ship was listing to starboard due to refuelling and taking on tons of water in preparation for departure to the Caribbean the next day. The guests, some seated at tables and others at the bars, were careful where they placed their drinking glasses, and those dancing were laughing about the novelty of adjusting to a slope of about three degrees. Social dancing was fun at walking pace, but Betty and I were powering round the floor, spinning in the waltz, stretching out in the slow foxtrot and executing staccato stop-starts in the tango without losing our balance – uphill, downhill and sideways. Big applause. Pausing for breath and mopping my brow with a white handkerchief, I turned to the band leader, Gilly Hulme: "Gilly, please let's canter, not gallop the quickstep and Viennese Waltz." We managed to stay upright, but even today we remember that performance as being 'very hard work'.

The majority of our engagements were at Southampton's Guildhall and the Polygon Hotel, most often dancing to the music of Bert Osborne's orchestra. National dance bands were hired for some of the major functions at the Guildhall: Betty and I had the privilege to give dance exhibitions to the music of Victor Silvester's strict-tempo orchestra, the big-band sound of the popular Joe Loss, the Latin American style of Edmundo Ross and Ivy Benson's wonderful All Girls Band. The scene: huge empty floor, big audience, big band, Betty's big dress, big applause – especially after we had accelerated round that vast space dancing an athletic quickstep.

On one occasion at the Polygon Hotel the organisers had booked three acts. Preceded by a conjuror, we were the last to perform. Bert Osborne announced us, and his band played our entry music. We flowed onto the dance floor, Betty spun round and round, her voluminous dress creating air waves before cascading around her onto the floor. Those air waves disturbed streamers and other debris created by the conjuror so I insisted on the floor being swept before we carried on. Two staff armed with yard-wide brooms appeared, then Bert's boys played our entry music again. We danced a waltz to 'Charmaine', the foxtrot to 'Unforgettable', tango to 'La Compasita' and the quickstep to 'Let's Face the Music and Dance'.

Preparing for a fast 'twinkle-toes' quickstep across the long, diagonal dimension of the floor I led Betty into multiple spins in one corner then set off at high speed. Suddenly, after a few steps, my right heel trod on half a walnut shell and I went down – well, my right knee collapsed to the floor while I held on tight to Betty's right hand in ballroom hold and, between gritted teeth, commanded without expletives, "Keep going, keep going." To some in the audience it may have looked as though I was proposing ... at that speed? The initial momentum and Betty's skill enabled me to slide all the way to the corner, spring upright, complete multiple spins to re-engage with our routine and, to great applause, continue the performance.

Some friends attending the function commented on the wonderful new sequence of steps we had introduced in our quickstep; evidently hardly anyone in the audience knew that I had trodden on a walnut shell. Twenty years later I was invited to make a speech at a corporate function in the Polygon Hotel. On walking into the lobby a couple approached me and said, "Oh Mr Rayment, so good to see you after all these years. Do you remember when you stepped on the walnut during your dance exhibition with Betty?"

*

Hampshire's last away match in 1956 was in Nottingham, where heavy rain wiped out play on the second day. Some of the team passed the time by going to the cinema, where the main feaure was 'Rock Around The Clock'.

> It was extraordinary. They had to stop the film because people were dancing in the aisles. Straightaway afterwards, I rang home to Betty. "We've got to do this," I said.

We went up to Kingston to learn all the throws, and we put a rock'n'roll act together. Instead of doing the Viennese waltz for our encore, we would race off into the Green Room, rip off the tails and dress, put on a sporty outfit and come out to do a rock'n'roll act, with the band playing 'Rock Around The Clock' and 'See You Later, Alligator'.

At the Grosvenor Ballroom Thursday was our dead night. People were paid, cash in a packet, on Friday, and very little happened on Thursday. So we decided to put on a rock'n'roll class and advertised it in the *Echo*. We were expecting about twenty people.

Just before eight o'clock, when the class was due to start, I was having a fag and a cup of coffee in the Bamboo Bar. I had been doing private lessons for three or four hours, and I was relaxing. I was inside the bar, and I heard the high heels of one of the students, Ann, coming up the stairs. She said, "Alan, will you come and see Betty? She is getting very worried what to do about letting people in." A lot of kidding went on between us, and I said, "Oh come on, Ann, pull the other one. Tell Betty I'll come when I've had another cigarette."

She went back down, and then male footsteps came up: David, the manager. "Betty's getting in a real panic," he said. I still thought they were pulling my leg. "Take it easy," I said. "There's nothing to worry about." So David went back, and next thing it's clack-clack-clack-clack, clack-clack-clack-clack: Betty, with the fast pace of her high heels. All fiery, eyes popping out. "You've got to come down now, Alan. I don't know what to do." Real panic.

There were 185 people queuing outside the front door, and there were four of us to teach them.

At half a crown each, the takings were £23 2s 6d, the equivalent of three full weeks of Alan's pay from Hampshire.

We were booked to give an exhibition in the upper-floor restaurant in Mayes department store. Two pillars in the middle of the relatively small dance floor restricted the flow of our routine. Fellow professionals used to joke, "Mayes? Do a feather and three-step and you are down the lift shaft if you're not careful."

We managed all right with our ballroom dances, but our rock'n'roll routine included throws, pull-throughs and lifts, one where Betty's legs went high in the air as she vaulted my bent back.

Introducing the new dancing

Betty's feet crashed into a ceiling chandelier, shattering the light bulbs and scattering glass, sizeable glass beads and bent wire over the dance floor. There were 'ooohs' and 'ahhhs' from the audience but, without stopping, we continued our performance on a clear patch of the floor. The show must go on! Huge applause.

Dancing at Mayes – and cricket, too. Together with my Hampshire county colleagues I remember batting and bowling on a matting wicket surrounded by a full net set up on the flat roof of the department store. I cannot remember the purpose of the event. Probably, though rare in the 1950s, a sales promotion for the store.

Hampshire's cricketers on the roof of Mayes department store

Alan and Betty were living life to the full, and the money was flowing in. Early in 1957 they bought a five-bedroom house in Brookvale Road in the leafy northern suburb of Highfield. Its previous owner was the Chief Engineer at Cunard, and it was a condition of the sale that they kept on his housekeeper Ivy. With Betty's mother Nellie also living with them, they had plenty of support at home, allowing them to throw themselves with great energy into their dance business.

I think my cricket did suffer a bit – but not my enthusiasm for it.

11

Cricket every day
1956 – 1957

The Hampshire fixture list for 1956 consisted of 31 first-class matches, each of three days' duration, and five friendlies: four of two days, one of three. From the start of their first friendly on Monday 30 April to the close of their last championship match on Tuesday 4 September, excluding Sundays, they were scheduled to play on 104 out of 110 days.

The first four in the Hampshire batting order – Roy Marshall, Jimmy Gray, Henry Horton and Alan – appeared in all 31 first-class matches. Key players were rested from some of the friendlies, but Alan and Henry Horton were excused from only one such match, a two-day game against the Royal Navy. As a boy at Finchley Alan's dream had been to play cricket every day, and between 9 June and 4 September 1956, bar Sundays, he did just that: 81 days in a row. Add in the travelling – at one point, driving from Southampton to Westcliff in Essex, up to Hull, then back to Southampton, all on pre-motorway roads – and it was a demanding schedule.

Yet there was no thought that the programme needed slimming down. Quite the contrary. In 1960 the counties were given the option to play either 28 or 32 championship matches, and Hampshire chose the latter, adding in games against the touring South Africans and both universities. There was not a single day's break in their schedule, with the journeys worse than in 1956: Swansea to Romford, Liverpool to Portsmouth, Bradford to Bournemouth.

A close-knit group of men, together day after day, needed the right mix of cheerful characters, and undoubtedly Alan's positive personality, combined with his outstanding fielding in the covers, kept him in the side. Despite playing all 31 first-class matches in 1956 he scored only four fifties, reaching his 1,000 runs in the last game when, starting on 997, he was dismissed for 2 and 1. Yet, as always, there were days when he shone brightly: a 'forceful' 94 against Gloucestershire at Southampton, a 'stubborn' 85 to prevent defeat by Essex at Westcliff, an 'aggressive' 71 against Somerset at Taunton and, best of all, a 'terrific' 65* against Warwickshire at Portsmouth when he defied the drizzle to secure an against-the-odds victory in a run chase.

Alan, Jimmy Gray and Vic Cannings

Hampshire did not repeat the success of their third place in 1955, dropping to sixth. The weather played its part in that, with rain ruining more of their matches than those of the teams which finished above them – and sixth was, after all, their second best finish since 1914. With a young team the county had every reason to remain in good spirits.

Chief among those who created a lively spirit in the dressing room was Vic Cannings, a down-to-earth character from the little village of Bighton between Winchester and Alton. He was 37 years old in the summer of 1956, and he lived for another 60 years, retaining a zest for life into his nineties. Alan was fascinated by Vic and arranged for me to visit him at the Eton College house where he had been allowed to stay on after the end of his 25 years as the school's cricket professional.

He was nearly 91 years old but, in his spritely movement and his mental alertness, he seemed more like 71. "If it weren't for my knees, I could still be bowling," he said, and for four hours he talked with vigour, brimming with the stories of his life. I suspect he would happily have gone on for another four hours, but it was six o'clock, his son and granddaughter were coming round to play mahjongg, and he had to cook them a meal.

I went back three months later, when he was a special guest at the Eton-Charterhouse match, and I witnessed the magnetic force of his personality at the lunch table, how everybody, the women especially, were drawn towards him. Alan had talked to me about this, how he had always had a way with women.

He had made no effort to acquire the accent or the ways of the upper class. Rather the opposite, he was still a farm worker's son or, as he put it, 'a little ragged-arsed bloke from the depths of Hampshire'. His predecessor at Eton, Essex's Jack O'Connor, had 'known his place', but that was not Vic's way.

> When I came to Eton I thought, they've got to take me as I am. Maybe I don't talk the proper English as they do, but we got by. They've always been good to me. Never paid me enough, mind you.
>
> Jack used to call the boys 'sir', but I said, "I'm not going to call any boy 'sir'." I swore at some of them. I called them Dick or Tom. The only one I didn't was Prince Richard of Gloucester. I'd talk to him without saying anything. Not that he played cricket.

Vic had spent his winters in the 1950s coaching overseas: in South Africa, Argentina, Trinidad, even Pakistan, though the last of these postings came to an abrupt end when his agreed pay did not materialise.

> The High Commissioner in Karachi said, "It would be nice if you could improve relations between our two countries, Mr Cannings." I said, "It would be nice for relations if I could be paid some money."

MCC's Billy Griffith recommended him to Eton. He and Surrey's Tom Clark were the best two men for the job, he said, with Vic the number one. So what qualities, I wondered, were they looking for? "A bloody idiot, I should think," he said. "It was back in the days of the bow and arrow."

> David McIndoe, the cricket master, said to me, "Obviously we like to win, but I want you to make them enjoy playing cricket." And that was what I tried to do in my stupid way. Have a bit of fun.
>
> I used to say to them, "Take no notice of what the master tells you. You do what I bloody tell you. And you'll get no bloody praise from me. I shall moan at you. And the better player you are, the more I shall moan. But I won't let any other bugger moan at you."

> The old boys come back, and they mimic me: "Worst bloody players I've ever had" in my Hampshire accent. The mothers used to say, "We've heard of you, Mr Cannings." And I'd say, "Nothing any good, I'll bet."

The boys all loved him, of course. I knew that from John Barclay, who had played in Vic's Eton eleven for four years. It was hard not to be captivated by his undimmed spirit. He was nobody's fool, and he went through life without affectation or pretence, just being himself.

At the age of 18, while working a ten-hour day on a lathe for an engineering firm, cycling nine miles each way in all weathers, he answered an advertisement in the *Sunday People* for recruits for the Palestine Police, spending the war years in the Middle East, in the midst of the conflict between the Arabs and the Jews. It was dangerous work with shootings and bombings – "We were trying to catch Menachem Begin, and we never did" – but he did not regret his decision. "I had the time of my life out there," he said. He played plenty of cricket, on artificial pitches, including two-day 'Test matches' against the Australians stationed there. Among them was Lindsay Hassett, Bradman's successor as Australian captain.

> He got 110 in the first innings. That evening we went down to the Police Club, tried to get him drunk, but the next day he got runs again. It made no difference.

Hassett wrote to him in February 1945, "from somewhere in the Pacific", and the letter turned up at his house in Eton in the 1960s. "I wrote back to him. 'It's about time I answered this letter,' I said." He was full of such stories.

Back in England in 1946 he went for a trial with Hampshire and was told there was no money, come back next year. Then to Glamorgan for whom he got four cheap wickets in a 2nd XI game on Barry Island but was told by letter that they were looking for batsmen. A major who had been in Palestine introduced him to Warwickshire who took him on after a trial match in which he had been given almost no opportunity to show his ability. A fellow recruit was Alan Townsend from Middlesbrough, who had scored a fifty in the game on Barry Island. His rejection letter from Glamorgan had said they were looking for bowlers. Such was the ramshackle way counties were rebuilding after the war.

Vic proudly listed the four centuries he had scored in minor matches, one in Nazareth. His highest first-class score was 61, his only fifty, for Warwickshire against Nottinghamshire – and that, too, had a story.

> I can't remember whether I was dropped six times and caught the seventh or dropped seven and caught the eighth. And they didn't have to move for any of them. Eventually Charlie Harris – mad as a hatter, Charlie was – he caught me in the gully. "I got him," he said, and he ran all round the pitch saying "I got him." Apparently they'd dropped 18 the week before at Gravesend.
>
> It was fun in those days, believe you me.

Finally in 1950, not having made it as a regular first-teamer at Warwickshire, he was playing for Hampshire, the county of his birth.

> Pre-season, when I ran in to bowl in the nets at Southampton, something was wrong. I didn't feel right. I asked some of the others, and they said this and that. Eventually I went over to Arthur Holt. He gathered up six balls and took me to a net on its own. I bowled one ball, and he said straightaway, "I think I've seen it. Go back and bowl another one." Apparently my front arm was bent; it wasn't bringing me round. I don't know how many people would have spotted that; the others didn't.
>
> He was bloody great, Arthur. He wasn't a great player, but he was one of the best three coaches in the game. I assume that somewhere there were another two!

At Hampshire Vic formed a decade-long partnership with Derek Shackleton:

> Neither of us was fast, not by present-day standards. I should think I was something like Collingwood, 71 to 73 miles an hour. Shack would have been 77 to 79. But we were both accurate. We said as a joke, if Shack bowled more than one half-volley a season, they would sack him, and I was allowed two.
>
> We never had any arguments. I liked to bowl up a slope, he liked to bowl down. I bowled away swing, he bowled in. So we never wanted the same end – except if a certain umpire was standing. For some reason he liked me; he'd give me anything. Shack would say, "I suppose you're going that end." I said, "Not half. That's worth two wickets, that is." I always made sure I walked out with him. We were at Bournemouth for the last game of one season. He said to me, "Have you got your 100 wickets yet?" And I said, "No." He said, "How many do you need?" I said, "Four." He said, "You get two, I'll get you the other two."
>
> My 100th was an lbw – but from the other umpire, thank God!

Such statistics could be an entertaining side-show during the season. In 1953 Australia's Bill Johnston, batting at number eleven, was caught and bowled by Vic – "a little dolly catch" – and the significance of the dismissal grew as the summer neared its end. By his last match at Hastings Johnston had batted 17 times for 102 runs, and he had only been out that once. As a result he stood on the verge of being only the second man, after Don Bradman, to end an English season with a batting average of 100 or more.

> I sent a telegram to Hastings. I said, "For Christ's sake, don't get out now, Bill. We'll both go down in posterity." And he didn't get out.

But it wasn't all laughter. He told me of a spat with David Sheppard – "I'm probably the only cricketer who's had a bishop apologise to him" – and of a day at Old Trafford when his fiery side got the better of him.

> Shack and I bowled our hearts out to keep the runs down, and Desmond Eagar was talked into making an early declaration. We lost the game, and we got cheered off for being sporting.
>
> In the dressing room I threw my boot at him. It only just missed, and I thought it would be the end of me. But Reg Dare said, "You know Vic, he's got a bit of a temper." And it blew over.

In truth, Vic was too valuable to the side to be lost on account of a flying boot, and Desmond Eagar was wise enough to know it – and to recognise how integral to the spirit of the team the 'ragged-arsed' Vic was.

*

The summer of 1957, the last of Desmond Eagar's twelve as captain, was a disappointing one, both for the county who finished 13th and for Alan. In preparation for taking over from Eagar, Colin Ingleby-Mackenzie was invited to play the full season and, when all the batsmen were fit, Alan found himself out of the side. His brief notes on the summer record few highlights:

> Did not play 1st XI until mid-June. Scored 80 v Notts at Cowes. Captained a strong Hampshire side v Army at Southampton and took four for 75 v Cambridge University, including Ted Dexter. However, only 659 runs ... was I more focused on family and business than cricket?

Their match against Surrey at Guildford coincided with celebrations to mark the 700th anniversary of the granting of a royal charter to the borough. On the second afternoon the Queen and Prince Philip visited the ground, but so speedily did Surrey beat Hampshire that by the time of their arrival the

Desmond Eagar presents the Hampshire team to the Queen and Prince Philip – The Queen is shaking hands with Alan

teams were playing an exhibition match. The huge crowd enjoyed some big hitting while the Queen took tea in the sun. "This is much more fun than sitting in a stuffy box at Lord's," she said to the Mayor.

Some felt that Peter May, the Surrey captain, should have delayed his declaration to make sure the match lasted till their arrival, especially as three days earlier the royal couple had been deprived of a day at the Lord's Test because England, also captained by May, had already won. "This is the second time you've let me down," she told him.

Alan's contribution to the embarrassingly early finish was to be bowled second ball by Jim Laker. Nevertheless, the Surrey spinner found room in his column in the *Sunday People* to pay tribute to Alan:

> Alan Rayment, of Hampshire, is one of the liveliest cover points in cricket. It's not surprising that he's so light on his feet. He and his wife, Betty, are a professional dancing team. They even have their own ballroom in Southampton. No wonder Alan is much in demand with those who fancy themselves at the 'light fantastic' whenever visiting teams are down Hampshire way.

Perhaps Alan was right. Perhaps the cricket was now taking second place to the dancing. In lesser matches he scored freely – 122* & 50 against Kent 2nd XI, 58 against The Army, 77 & 62 against Cambridge University – but his 28 innings in the county championship yielded only two fifties and four other scores over 25.

Yet Alan did not seem to worry unduly when he was in a bad run. He retained something of the amateur outlook of his early years at Finchley, living life to the full and enjoying it.

> I still loved being involved in all aspects of my summer occupation. When not in the Hampshire first team, or twelfth man, I was happy to play in the second eleven, sometimes as captain, and really enjoyed the friendly club cricketers I met when playing against Deanery, Trojans, Bournemouth Sports Club, Basingstoke, Lymington, Ventnor on the Isle of Wight and many others. The Kid who turned professional at the age of twenty was still a club cricketer at heart; the psychological imprint of my cricketing youth at Finchley's Arden Field was indelible. And the experience of teaching dancing and coaching cricket for nine years proved to be a parallel joy to the Young Kid's dream to 'play cricket every summer's day'.

Alan, with his profitable dance business and ever-upbeat approach to his cricket, was certainly different from his professional team-mates who, it seems, did not always know what to make of him. "Punchy? He was round the bend," was Vic Cannings' down-to-earth verdict on him. "We used to pick a Punchy XI, with Punchy as the skipper. Charlie Harris was in the team, and Dickie Dodds because he was a bit punchy, too. And a few others I can't remember."

*

That year Alan passed the examination to become a member of the National Association of Teachers of Dancing, and he also passed the Advanced Cricket Coaching Certificate, attending Lilleshall for the week with, among others, Godfrey Evans, Mike Smith and Peter Sainsbury. With his background in dance teaching, the course came easily to him.

> I already had that analytical mind about movement. It was no big deal. Somebody told me in confidence that my mark in the theory test was the highest they had ever awarded.

His career as a professional cricketer might not be fulfilling its early promise, but in so much of his life he was enthusiastically going forward. Or was he?

The MCC Advanced Coaching Certificate Course, Lilleshall, 1957
Alan is mid-picture, holding his bat with a high back lift.
On the back wall is Godfrey Evans. Top left with bat is Arthur Holt.

As Alan knew well, memories have a fluid quality, especially when they involve intense emotions. In November 1957 Alan suffered a shock that changed his life dramatically, a shock that turned his thinking upside down and led him down a road of spiritual quest that, to an extent, dominated the rest of his life. I may be wrong, but I am inclined to think that he would have ended up on that road sooner or later without the shock of that November. Nevertheless, it was the catalyst for an extraordinary change of direction, and it is not possible to complete this book without acknowledging it.

I think it is possible that, in seeking to make sense of what happened to him that November, Alan's emotional memory created too idyllic a picture of his life at that point. By his own admission he was absorbed fully with all the activities of his busy existence, failing to pay sufficient attention to what mattered most to him, and perhaps we need to remember this when we read his joyful description of the state of his life that autumn:

> As cooler days and shortened evenings once again confirmed the passing of the summer game – of running bending low to scoop the ball at cover point or bent at hips in stance to eye the bowler's flight – I stood up straight, or nearly so, to dance the waltz and teach the posture, poise and line of dancer's grace sought by female pupil seeking gold medallion in next month's medal test. I struggled, as always through September, to rebuild the abdominal core and lessen the active strength of shoulders and arms. Whilst team mates Henry, Jim and Mike changed professional working gear from white-spiked footwear to rounded studs on dubbined leather hard-toed boots, I slipped on patent black with chamois non-slip soles and told my legs to glide and not to run and pound the parquet floor of the Grosvenor Ballroom.
>
> Yet even more than the seasonal change of occupations I looked forward to unbroken weeks of family life with Betty and the children and in-house banter with Nellie and Ivy. Before Denis and Martin returned to school and Betty and I became immersed in a busy autumn programme of teaching and exhibitions, we enjoyed our first family holiday in eight years, leaving staff to run the business. We drove to a hotel for an overnight stay in Exeter, on through the scenic splendour of North Devon the next day and arrived safely at a guesthouse overlooking Woolacombe's sandy bay.

Now, over fifty years later, Betty and I laugh at the memory of packing three children and a few items of necessary holiday-wear plus buckets and spades into the back of our tiny Austin A35 van. Today, when daughter Angela and her three sons pack for a trip to their holiday home in Brittany, every inch inside their comparatively huge Citroen People Carrier is stuffed floor to roof.

The Devon countryside was glorious, the beaches seemingly endless, our hosts friendly and the weather capricious. We all revelled in the adventure – new scenes, new places, new faces and food. But all too soon Saturday was upon us and we piled into the little Austin to drive home to Highfield – refreshed and happy. Excited children plied Nellie and Ivy with tales of the trip while Betty checked school clothes for Monday and I visited the ballroom to check the week's business with David and Ann.

Business was booming and continued to boom through September and October. Ballroom classes averaged 35 pupils, rock'n'roll between 50 and 70, and a new class for business people attracted couples preparing for the seasonal round of dinner dances. I was fully booked for private tuition, Betty too in the time slots available when free from family duties. Our rehearsals for exhibitions at public functions had to be fitted into our busy weekly schedule in addition to an occasional lesson from a top professional in London or Guildford. Ballroom manager David had a full diary for private lessons, and student teacher Ann gave competent private tuition to a number of youthful beginners. Yes, we were all busy-busy and our finances healthy.

However, we had to set a new limit to the number of people attending our public dances on Saturday evenings. The rock'n'roll revolution was now in full swing, and each couple needed more floor space to strut their stuff – to perform hip lifts, 'through the legs' and 'over the top'. In the previous winter we could accommodate 350 dancers on Saturday evening: now we closed the doors when 250 had paid their entrance fee of five shillings. This meant an average reduction of £25 in our weekly takings which was partly balanced with a public dance on Wednesday evenings and a reduction of musicians from eleven to seven. For dance exhibitions at company dinner dances and civic events Betty and I charged 15 guineas.

In 1957 Hampshire paid me £500, and our net profit before tax from the Grosvenor Ballroom was £2,500. The business that Betty and I started in church halls in 1950 had, with hard work and often long hours, grown exponentially to produce an annual income five times greater than I received from cricket.

What a Life! What a very good life in every aspect. First and foremost, the well-being and all-round development of our children, Denis, Martin and Valerie, was our primary interest and responsibility. We lived in a relatively large house in a good neighbourhood. Our wonderful housekeeper, Ivy, covered all the basic duties, the laundry and the cooking as well being a caring member of the family. Fred, the part-time gardener, relieved me of pleasant jobs I did not have time to fulfil. Nellie was a capable, loving and unobtrusive grandmother whose live-in presence enabled Betty and me to cope with the unsocial hours of our business. David and Ann covered our absences from the ballroom when family duties took precedence over business.

Denis was well established at Oakmount School and proving himself to be intellectually bright, socially at ease, excellent at sport and a good singer. Martin, now approaching his fourth birthday, was sailing ahead at St Christopher's PNEU School. An avid reader, Martin read Guttenburg's New Testament before his fourth birthday and was seriously good with numbers, too. Valerie, a lively and lovely two-year-old, would attend nursery school after Christmas.

A happy family, living in some luxury by the standards of the time, and a thriving business. That is how Alan recalls it. But it was not, alas, the whole truth.

12

The tremendous mystery
November 1957

There was a prestige attached to being a county cricketer in the 1950s, and some made the most of this, taking the opportunities provided by away matches to enjoy the company of admiring women. Alan was not one of these, having a strong sense of his marriage vows which were reinforced when he and Betty were confirmed at All Saints Church in Millbrook.

Alan and Betty at the Grosvenor Ballroom in 1957

Betty, however, remained in the glamorous environment of the ballroom, and during the summer of 1957 a relationship of some significance developed in her life. Did Alan have any inkling of this? According to his notes for this chapter:

> In Sept and Oct I was, at times, 'uncomfortable'. On some days I felt mildly nauseous, but I was so busy at the ballroom and with the children. I began to have a feeling that something was not right.

A Hampshire committee member rang Alan at home on the afternoon of Guy Fawkes Night, spelling out what he and his friends had been observing. Alan, it seemed, had been so absorbed with his busy routine that he had not seen – or perhaps had not wanted to see – what was in plain view to many others. With his mind in a whirl he rang Betty at the ballroom, asking her not to come home that night.

> I held myself together for bonfire and firework duty with the children in our garden. Immediately after the children were asleep I collapsed onto our bedroom floor and wept.
>
> I was in shock and angry and so distraught that I 'emptied' myself through crying and an all-over pain I could not describe. I was like a punctured balloon, empty of life.

There followed an experience that changed his life, an experience that he tried to capture in words more than fifty years later, writing in the present tense in an attempt to recreate its immediacy:

> The pain in my head, heart and guts is almost unbearable. Flat on the floor, aching and empty, devoid of energy, unable to move or think, I remain motionless for a long long time until, from a neighbour's garden, a battery of fireworks – BANG BANG SPLUTTER BANG – jump-start an unexpected thought: GOD!
>
> Heaving my limp body to a kneeling position, I crawl across the carpet to the window facing Brookvale Road, grab the sill, pull myself up to a standing position and draw one curtain aside. Pitching my gaze above the light radiating from street lamps I emit a hoarse groan for help:
>
> "God ... if there is a God? *(big question mark)* ... please sort out this awful mess our lives are in." Then I collapse again to a prone position beside the dressing table where I remain for an indeterminate time until ... until, slowly, very slowly, I begin to feel a gentle energy entering my body ... as though a hand-pump has been attached to the deflated balloon. Every part of my body is being refreshed, slowly. I find myself thinking: "Is this God giving me strength? ... and now ... er ... something else ... feels like faith ... and ... er ... love ... I'm filling up and overflowing with Divine Love ... please stop, stop ... this is too much ... please, I am frightened!"
>
> Fear leaves me the instant I stand and move slowly around the bedroom. The Energy ... The Love and Peace Beyond Understanding

fills me – and fills the whole room – the soft warm light that pervades the room seems linked with the glow within me. I kneel to pray, to talk with The Presence – my mind alight with questions, my body pulsating with a calm energy emanating from an even deeper inner peace.

Everything around me in the room is normal, but I sense I'm experiencing another level of Life – my 'senses' are acute – I see and hear, know and understand ... *beyond words*! Bursting with wonder and thankfulness I sing, softly, sometimes humming, Hallelujah ... Hallelujah ... Hal ... layhay ... lu-hu ... jah!! – on and on and on ... my words combining with the music of a full orchestra and chorus in my head. Time evaporates – seems endless. I wake before dawn, laying on the bed fully clothed.

He showered and dressed, his mind racing with questions.

Do I live in two places at one and the same time? Everything in this bedroom and the bathroom is the same as yesterday and yet different in some way. And I am the same Alan as yesterday – but I am not: I feel a calm, vibrant physical energy I have not known before, and my mind is a relative powerhouse. Yesterday the totally unexpected capsize that almost drowned me: today, though my heart is aching, a renewed confidence that we will repair the family boat and sail on into the wind. I'm having a moment of enlightenment, but there is so much – more than ever before – that I *do not understand.* Paradox upon paradox. I need to read something ... What about a bible?

It was 6.30 in the morning, and he tiptoed down the stairs to look for his bible in the study.

On entering the room I was stilled into open-mouthed awe: the roses were *alight*. Seven large deep crimson roses from the garden displayed in a wide-necked vase on a low coffee table were *shimmering*, exuding a multi-hued glow. I paused to absorb the extraordinary sight. Beautiful, so beautiful – a heavenly sign? I knew nothing of auras and could only think of Moses and the burning bush.

This was a little scary, and I so needed to understand what was happening to me. 'Where the heck is that bible?' Found, under the magazines. I returned to the bedroom and devoured several chapters of John's gospel, amazed that I was reading so fast and that I was able to comprehend the text with an intellectual depth I had not known before.

The intensity of it all was broken finally by the arrival in the bedroom of two-year-old Valerie.

She bounced on the bed and asked, "Where's Mummy?"

*

For Alan there were two priorities. First, his family which he was desperate to reunite. Second, his need to make sense of his experience that night.

> That quest became a pilgrimage threading through the tapestry of daily living for the next 25 years. But in November 1957 I desperately wanted to know NOW. But how? And who would understand?
>
> I poured out my story to the Rector of Highfield Church, the Reverend Michael Couper, a kind and learned man. He listened, empathised, seemed puzzled, offered no answers but suggested some books to read. His parting words annoyed me: "Alan, you may be at the beginning of a very long journey."
>
> I did not even grasp that his words might be prophetic: I wanted answers, NOW! I marched round the corner of Brookvale Road into Portswood's shopping area, entered a small second-hand bookshop and purchased two religious books – one being 'Mere Christianity' by CS Lewis, an author of whom I knew nothing. But glancing through the chapter headings gave me hope that I would find some answers. I was thirsting for *answers!*

In the next days he worked through both the New Testament and 'Mere Christianity'.

> Spiritually and intellectually I was buzzing: part lifted up and satisfied; part burgeoning with curiosity and wanting more-more; part dissatisfied because I still had no definitive answers as to what had happened and was still *happening* to me. Who could I talk to, who would listen and hopefully understand, who might have some answers – at least a few – to my many questions?
>
> How about David Sheppard?

On the morning of Friday 15 November, with the same impetuosity that led him in the summer of 1948 to catch a train to Hove to seek out Patsy Hendren, Alan delegated all his tasks for the day and boarded a train to London in search of David Sheppard. What followed was another experience that left a lifelong impression on him:

I sat at a table in the rear of an open carriage looking out of the window, observing the suburban and rural scenes, until we stopped at Winchester. Four matronly ladies, two wearing fur coats, settled round a table in my eye-line further up the carriage and ordered tea and toast from the attendant. Likewise, I ordered a pot of tea, opened the CS Lewis book at page 121 but resumed gazing through the window, thinking about the dramatic changes in my life.

Slowly and gently I began to feel The Presence within and around me – and softly spoken words: "Look halfway down the page if you are in doubt that I am beside you instead of out the window … Could you talk to me from out there?" Surprised but calm, I looked down at the book open on the table, placed my finger on the second paragraph of the chapter 'Making and Begetting' and read the words:

> In a way I quite understand why some people are put off by Theology. I remember once when I had been giving a talk to the R.A.F. an old, hard bitten officer got up and said, "I've no use for all that stuff. But, mind you, I'm a religious man, too. I know there's a God. I've felt Him: out alone in the desert at night: the tremendous mystery. And that's just why I don't believe all your neat little dogmas and formulas about Him. To anyone who's met the real thing they all seem so petty and pedantic and unreal!"

I read the passage again: "Thank You." I felt an indescribable peace and, in a similar way to the experience on November 5, Time seemed to slow down as the Divine Presence filled me, then slowly expanded beyond my space, further and further into the carriage, causing me to plead, "Please, God, this is so embarrassing … please go away." And again … and again, because I noticed one of the fur-coated ladies was staring in my direction. I was sure she was spiritually sensitive and felt, or could even 'see' the change in the energy permeating our coach.

As the train eased into Basingstoke station the expanded energy of The Presence faded; my embarrassment ceased; I felt encapsulated in a peaceful cocoon of love – and something that I can only describe as mysterious certainty. Again, an experience *beyond words*.

Jolted back to the reality of the here and now by the click-clack of carriage doors and the hubbub of children's voices scrambling into seats nearby, I poured tepid tea from the pot and returned to page 121 to re-read the words of 'the old R.A.F. officer'. I wished I could meet him – or anyone who had 'experienced the real thing'.

Before alighting at Waterloo station I wrote a note in the margin of page 121 with my fountain pen:

15.11.57. TO LONDON ON TRAIN. FELT GOD'S PRESENCE. HE SAID 'LOOK HALF WAY DOWN THIS PAGE IF YOU ARE IN DOUBT THAT I AM BESIDE YOU INSTEAD OF OUT OF THE WINDOW. COULD YOU TALK TO ME FROM OUT THERE'

Recently, I discovered the British Transport Catering Services receipt tucked under the inside flap of the dust jacket of 'Mere Christianity'. Tea 1/6d.

At Waterloo station Alan found himself 'steered' to a bench next to an elderly lady, bedraggled and homeless.

I listened to her long, sad story and encouraged her that God was real and loved her. When we said goodbye fifty minutes later her eyes were brighter, and she blew me a kiss as I walked towards the taxi rank. I now felt elated but vulnerable. I doubted that I could cope with another 'close encounter'.

Arriving at David Sheppard's front door, he was met by a housekeeper. "I'm sorry," she said. "The Reverend Sheppard and his wife are away." Alan pleaded to know where he was, but she remained firm: "I'm really sorry, Mr Rayment, but I have strict instructions not to divulge his whereabouts."

"But ... but I have travelled all the way from Southampton ... Would you mind phoning for a taxi to take me back to Waterloo?"

The housekeeper gave an involuntary gasp, put her hand to her mouth and uttered, "Oh! They are in Lyndhurst." "Where in Lyndhurst?" I enquired politely. "I really don't know, Mr Rayment. In one of the hotels, I suppose."

And so ensued the fastest trip from North London to the New Forest I have ever made. Taxi to Waterloo station; phone call to Peter Sainsbury. Yes, I could borrow his car and yes, he would meet me at Southampton station in two hours – which he did and, bless him, said he would catch a bus home. I drove Pete's roly-poly Standard Vanguard at speed past Totton and through Ashurst, pulled into the Park Hotel, ran to the reception desk and enquired whether the Reverend Sheppard was a guest. No.

I received a negative response at three other hotels in the centre of Lyndhurst, made enquiries at the last one regarding quiet hotels in the surrounding countryside and eventually discovered David and Grace in a hotel on the Beaulieu Road.

David met me in the reception lobby. He looked serious and worried, stated that Grace was unwell and that he could not talk with me that day. However, he graciously accepted an invitation to visit me at Brookvale Road before they returned to Islington. I thanked him, wished Grace a speedy recovery, drove 'roly-poly' sedately through the Forest and returned the almost brakeless Vanguard to Pete's house. "Many thanks, Sains, you're a real pal. Think you'd better get a mechanic to look at the brakes."

The following Wednesday the Sheppards arrived at Alan's house.

We shared warm greetings in the spacious hall, and I remember that their body language revealed their surprise at my worldly status as evidenced by the size and quality of the house and furnishings. How could this be? I was a professional cricketer earning £500 a year.

Having ushered my guests to a settee in the lounge, I popped into the kitchen and asked Ivy to bring us a pot of tea in half an hour, with some biscuits or cake.

Alan found it hard to recall the occasion without chuckling about the performance of Ivy, his housekeeper. Nellie, Betty's mother, had moved in elite circles in her Edwardian youth and decided that it would be appropriate if Ivy put on a show for their distinguished visitors.

A knock on the door: "Come in." Ivy entered, carrying a large tray on which I was surprised to see an ornate silver tea-pot set, together with some posh teacups, saucers, plates and cake knives that I knew belonged to Nellie. I was even more surprised – open-mouthed, in fact – to see Ivy dressed in a maid's outfit replete with frilly white head-band, resurrected from duties with the previous owners of the house. I introduced Ivy, thanked her for the tea and cakes, whereupon she asked, "Will there be anything else, sir?"

To Alan's great disappointment David and Grace Sheppard could not provide the answers he was seeking.

> They were both concerned and empathic regarding the marital crisis and the effect on the children but uneasy when I spoke about my experiences of The Presence. David took a small book from his jacket pocket and asked if I ever read the bible. I replied that I had powered my way through the New Testament in recent days and, surprisingly, had been helped and even inspired by much of what I read. But my most important and pressing need was to understand the 'experiences' that had happened – and were still happening – since my cry for help: "God – if there is a God?"
>
> David's manner was warm and friendly, but he seemed uncomfortable with my 'What's it all about?' direct questions and stonewalled on matters he regarded as mystical. I became quietly frustrated as he diverted my questions to his opinions, which were mostly about the value of bible study, and made a strong recommendation that I should join an evangelical Anglican church.

With the support of Nellie and Ivy, the routine of home life was maintained, though the children were unsettled, repeatedly asking, "When will Mummy be better and come home?" Then, at the end of the month, Betty rang to say that she had talked it all through with friends and also with David Sheppard, and she wanted to come back and make a fresh start.

> My new faith gave me an inner strength and coping abilities without which I would have collapsed. Healing the surface emotions took time, the deeper-repressed wounds many years. But in the 'now' of late November 1957 the practical routines of family life were restored. Worried frowns disappeared from the faces of Denis, Martin and Valerie as they readily responded to the love of two truly caring parents.

13

Into the unknown
1958

The first priority for Alan and Betty, in the aftermath of their tumultuous November, was to re-establish the routine of their lives, to keep the ballroom and the dance exhibitions going and, above all, to reassure the children of their parents' togetherness.

> We were Mum and Dad, and they were dependent on us in most aspects of their lives. We truly loved them and would always strive to do our best for them. But we had messed up, taken our eyes off the ball, failed to discuss our individual needs and aspirations at a deep level. We were both too young, too naive and had too little understanding of many aspects of life, especially relationships. We lacked awareness of the degree to which rapid social change was affecting our life journey.

The routines were restored, both at home and also at work, where the dance teaching continued to be in great demand. Yet, for Alan, there remained the need to understand his experiences on Guy Fawkes' Night and on the train to London. He read and re-read the New Testament, especially chapters 14 and 15 of John's Gospel; he attended Holy Communion at Highfield Church; he prayed at home; and he asked searching questions of Dr Alan Oakley-John, a lay reader at Holy Saviour Church in Bitterne, and Leith Samuel, minister at the Above Bar Free Evangelical Church.

Alan's experiences were not a recognisable part of the theology of mainstream Anglicanism, nor was there a home for them in the increasingly influential Evangelical Movement of which David Sheppard was a part and which Billy Graham was popularising. His experiences would have been recognised and understood by members of the Charismatic Movement, but in 1958 that was still in its infancy in America, yet to reach Britain.

> I needed, almost desperately, to talk with a person or persons who would listen non-judgementally, help me with answers to at least some of my questions and even share with me their own 'mystical'

experiences. Surely some church-going Christians had experienced *The Presence*. But no one in Highfield Church or associated with Leith Samuel or Dr Alan tuned in to me; some backed off as though I had scared them or thought I was loony.

In January I attended a bible study at the home of a Bitterne parishioner and met about twenty kindly, middle-class people who were all really friendly towards me. I am guessing that as a Hampshire cricketer I was afforded a social status that was acceptable. After the study period the ladies set out refreshments in the dining room while the men stayed in the lounge discussing the sins of drinking alcohol and smoking. By admitting to both I stirred Puritan prejudices and made it clear that I didn't think such things mattered to God though in excess they might not be good for the health of we mere mortals. On entering the dining room I stopped and stared; never before had I witnessed such a display of cream-cake gluttony piled high on a score of plates. I was too shocked and too polite to say anything, but I learnt a lesson about 'motes and beams'.

A few weeks later my thirst to understand was partly assuaged when, with the same group, I attended a weekend workshop on the subject of evangelism led by the Reverend Canon Raymond Scantlebury. His expositions on bible texts were both spiritual and down to earth, wise and worldly, positive and sprinkled with humour. I liked him and cornered him for a short private chat at the end of the session. He listened, was empathic and suggested we should meet for a longer talk in the near future. I suggested that I visit him by appointment, then became discouraged when he told me his home was in Carlisle.

Nothing was going to hold Alan back, however, and he duly rang the Canon to make an appointment. As it happened, Peter Sainsbury was going to be driving that day to the Midlands, to meet up with his friend from National Service days, Tom Cartwright, and Alan travelled with him, parting at Birmingham's New Street Station. Unfortunately Alan had not studied the railway timetable and, underestimating the distance, did not arrive in Carlisle till 9.30 in the evening.

As with his trip to London to see David Sheppard, there was an otherworldliness about Alan's quest, but he was not disheartened, booking into a hotel and ringing the Canon to rearrange his appointment for the next day.

And, as with the homeless lady on the bench at Waterloo, he found himself drawn into conversation with a troubled stranger.

> Before going to my room I left my suitcase with the porter and, needing a drink and a sandwich, entered the public bar – a long room with a long bar, at the other end of which two men were having a loud argument over their respective claims to the services of a mature prostitute. As I ordered half a pint of Guinness I experienced a really strong *nudge* and the words: "Intervene and restore peace." "What?! … Oh no, that's asking too much … too embarrassing and frightening."
>
> I felt emboldened by a strange strength within and around me and, though at the same time feeling nervous, edged my way slowly down the bar until I reached the trio, lit a cigarette and offered to buy them a drink. I have no recollection of the conversation but succeeded, to my surprise, in calming the situation and negotiating an agreement that the chap in a dark blue suit would leave with the woman and I would have a chat with the more inebriated, cloth-capped Geordie. I listened as Tom, an unemployed high-level steel worker, unloaded problem after problem in a semi-coherent manner until I suggested that we meet the next morning in a cafe near the station. I collected my suitcase and bedroom key, climbed the stairs and flopped onto the bed, feeling elated and amazed, my mind buzzing and flowing with questions.
>
> I sat up and began to pray, asking 'Why?' to every aspect of the encounter in the hotel bar with the emphasis on 'Why me?' The silent response was overwhelming. There followed a period of immeasurable time, again beyond words to describe, as *The Presence* began to fill me and expand throughout the room. I laid prostrate on the floor in awe and reverence as *Divine Love, Extreme Joy* and *Peace Beyond Understanding* flowed through my whole Being. I asked 'Why?' and received, 'No reason, only knowing that you and I are One.'
>
> I woke at three in the morning, surprised to find myself lying on the floor in an unfamiliar room – fully dressed, feeling rested and calm. Then I remembered. I jumped up, found the wash basin, splashed cold water over my face, looked around the room … then at myself in the dressing-table mirror. A familiar face but an unfamiliar warm and peaceful glow within. Yes, I was feeling the afterglow of

an encounter with the Divine Presence – as I had at home and on the train in November. As I changed into pyjamas and pulled back the bedding I was humming the Hallelujah Chorus. I read myself to sleep, meditating on passages in chapter 14 of John's Gospel.

While writing the above in 2014, I felt a need to check the biblical passage and discovered, to my amazement, the following margin note written with a fountain pen against chapter 14, verse 21 in the tattered and much-marked King James Bible that I used for a few years from 5 November 1957:

24/2/58 Room 156 CROWN & MITRE CARLISLE

Verse 27 is also underlined with the same pen and colour ink: words deeply meaningful, following the first experience and throughout the last 57 years in times of struggle or confusion or joy.

> *Peace I leave with you, my peace I give unto you: not as the world giveth, give I unto you. Let not your heart be troubled, neither let it be afraid.*

To his surprise, when Alan arrived at the cafe next morning, Tom was waiting for him. After several cups of tea they walked to a park by the river and found a quiet bench where Tom poured out his troubles: his alcoholism, his inability to hold down jobs, the breakup of his marriage, how he missed his children.

Tom talked, I listened and time flew by. Eventually I broached the subject of faith and religion. Tom had been brought up as a Catholic and, although he believed in God, he had rejected his Church because of all the rules and the emphasis on punishment for a multitude of sins. I mentioned that I had recently asked for God's help in a crisis and received an unexpected boost of strength and love that had pulled me through. Maybe he could also *ask* for help and *expect* to receive – directly as from a friend and not through a religious organisation.

Then they talked football: the recent Munich air crash in which so many Manchester United footballers had been killed and the Newcastle stars that Tom admired. Gradually Tom's Geordie humour surfaced, his broad dialect leaving Alan grasping little more than the expletives.

Although I felt inadequate in my knowledge and understanding of his alcoholism, my listening to his troubles had helped Tom become less anxious and think more positively about his near future, in particular to ask for help from his doctor or visit a hospital as an outpatient.

It was afternoon by the time Alan reached the Scanteburys' house.

Raymond and his wife, Margaret, were in their early fifties, a warm and friendly couple, theologically on the liberal evangelical wing of the Anglican church, worldly-wise and possessing a natural sense of humour.

I apologised for my delayed arrival, which now made it more imperative for me to gain some understanding of three major mystical, or spiritual, experiences, even what to call those radical events that had occurred in November and the previous night. The kindly Canon ushered me into his study; the walls were lined with books I longed to investigate, but the business of the moment was to be conducted from a comfortable, well-worn, brown leather chair opposite his own well-cushioned twin.

I recounted my experience of November fifth in more detail; the 'happenings' on the train to Waterloo and the chat with the bedraggled lady on the station concourse; the visit to my home by David and Grace Sheppard; the surprising events in the Crown and Mitre Hotel and the subsequent meeting with Tom. Even the shortened versions of those stories took a while to recount. At the end I emphasised that my greatest need was to *understand*. Yes, I was thankful, yes I was in awe, yes I had been blessed with a deep inner peace ... but! So many 'buts' – and no person had given satisfactory answers to my many questions. And why did educated clergy and experienced Christians become so defensive, even back off and avoid me?

Canon Scantlebury listened attentively, empathised with my concern regarding the effects of the marital crisis on the children and reassured me that during his ministry he had met individuals who had received 'visitations' similar to mine. He said that the mystical aspects of the Christian faith had, historically, been controversial and in the modern era were disregarded by the main denominations. There were, however, several books written by men and women who had unexpectedly been 'baptised in the Spirit' and many books written early in the century on the subject of the Welsh Revival in 1904-05 and the birth of the Pentecostal Movement in Los Angeles in 1906. Also, in a kindly pastoral way, the Canon counselled me to be selective regarding those with whom I shared my experiences and to find a bible-based church where I felt comfortable with the teaching and members of the congregation.

Although I felt heartened by their friendship and encouraged by the Canon's acceptance of the validity and normality of my experiences, my quest for *understanding* had not been satisfied during this meeting. But I remember him saying: "The Way for The Pilgrim is long and often hard."

I did not understand what he meant back then in 1958: I do now in 2014 as I review my journey – at least in part.

Now I know in part; then I shall understand fully,
even as I have been fully understood.

During the long train journey home to Southampton I had time to think, to write, to puzzle and to pray. I concluded that in the past few months I had passed through a GATEWAY INTO THE UNKNOWN.

*

Cricket began in May, with Alan scoring runs in the warm-up matches. It was the first year of Colin Ingleby-Mackenzie's captaincy, and before they travelled north for the first three championship matches the 24-year-old skipper gathered the team together to give them a 'pep talk', the theme of which was "Let's enjoy the game." His concluding words – "Win or lose, let's entertain or perish" – suggested a more cavalier approach than his predecessor.

This approach could hardly have got off to a worse start. At Bradford, in a match reduced by rain to one day, he unwisely opted to bat first and compounded his error by declaring too early, leaving Yorkshire 106 to win in 55 minutes, a task he assumed would be impossible against Shackleton and Heath. Then, to the amazement of all, Freddie Trueman came in at number four and blasted 58 in half an hour, mostly off the bewildered Shack, and the hosts won with five minutes to spare. 'As we left the field,' Ingleby-Mackenzie wrote in his autobiography, 'we were astonished to receive a reception greater than any we met until winning the championship three years later. The Yorkshire crowd stood and cheered as though we had won a great victory instead of putting up what I considered to be a fairly dismal exhibition and a monumental boob.'

Rare indeed were the occasions when batsmen collared Shackleton's bowling. Trueman did it again seven years later, hitting 26 in an over at

Middlesbrough when Shack's other 31 overs went for just 45 runs. The only other batsman whom Shack's Hampshire team-mates remembered taking such liberties was David Sheppard, who at Bournemouth once straight-drove the metronomic bowler for three sixes and a four in an over.

Heavy defeats followed at Trent Bridge and Old Trafford, and the Hampshire team returned south with no sense that their new skipper's "Let's enjoy the game" approach would generate success. 'I began to wonder whether we would ever win a match,' he wrote. 'Was the game really all the fun I had tried to tell the team we must make it?'

Their mood changed in the next match against Worcestershire at Portsmouth, and this was in no small part due to Alan, who played what he considered two of his best innings for Hampshire.

Vic Cannings, described by *The Times* as 'a cheerful performer who likes laughing', took six wickets in the visitors' first innings of 205, and in reply Roy Marshall hit a brisk 76. But, with rain interrupting the first two days, it was a 'delightful stand' between Alan (62) and his skipper (67) that allowed Ingleby-Mackenzie to make a surprise declaration before the close of the second day. Nevertheless, a result looked unlikely when Worcestershire batted past tea on the last day. When the final wicket fell, Hampshire needed 124 for victory in only 75 minutes – with Worcestershire's seam bowlers Flavell, Coldwell and Pearson all bowling off long runs to defensive fields.

To his surprise Alan was asked to go in first with Roy Marshall and, with the sun finally appearing to warm 'the hardy folk who had sat huddled in coats and mackintoshes throughout a chilly day', they had 37 runs on the board in five overs.

> Portsmouth was always a nice, hard wicket. I remember Flavell, he was red-headed and he got madder and madder.

After Marshall fell to a running catch, Mike Barnard joined Alan, and to great cheers the pair completed the victory with seven minutes to spare, Alan 'imperiously' sweeping the winning boundary to fine leg and sending 'Nomad' in the *Southern Echo* into ecstasy:

> There are few better things in county cricket than watching a side beat the clock in a dramatic victory as Hampshire did at Portsmouth yesterday ... Undoubtedly the man of the match was Rayment. His share of a triumph which I feel sure will boost the side's morale enormously was an unbeaten 72 out of 127 made in just 68 minutes – as fine an exhibition of hard but judicious hitting as I have ever

seen from a player who in recent years has sometimes failed to do himself justice ... It must have been a proud moment for Rayment as he and Barnard were applauded all the way back to pavilion, there to be greeted by their delighted captain.

Alan's superb knock did indeed raise morale, and the county went on to have the best season yet in its history, leading the table through July and most of August before finishing second to Surrey. However, for Alan, in the all too familiar pattern of his career, his triumph was followed by a succession of low scores – 5 & 4, 24 & 3, 3 & 2, 2 & 0 – till he was dropped in favour of the younger Ray Pitman. Only once, when Ingleby-Mackenzie and Marshall were away at the Gentlemen/Players match, did Alan return to the side, hitting a bright 40 against Gloucestershire at Southampton.

At Lord's, June 1958 – Alan's penultimate game for Hampshire
back: Arthur Holt (coach), Peter Sainsbury, Henry Horton, 'Butch' White, Malcolm Heath, Mike Barnard, Mervyn Burden (twelfth man), Norman Drake (scorer)
front: Alan Rayment, Derek Shackleton, Roy Marshall,
Colin Ingleby-Mackenzie (captain), Leo Harrison, Jimmy Gray

At the start of the summer Alan had told Hampshire he would not be available beyond that year; he had other plans for his life.

In ten seasons for the county he played in 198 matches and scored 6,333 runs at an average of 20.46, with four centuries and 23 fifties. He also took 19 wickets and held 86 catches.

As Alan knew only too well, his average did not do justice to his ability but, in fairness to him, these were mostly wet summers of three-day cricket played on uncovered pitches. Colin Ingleby-Mackenzie had a Hampshire average of 24.59, Mike Barnard 22.07, Desmond Eagar 21.02, Leo Harrison 17.66 and Ray Pitman 13.61. Only the very best of them – Neville Rogers, Roy Marshall, Henry Horton and Jimmy Gray – got into the 30s.

*

During August a young reporter interviewed Alan about his plans for the future. Recalling the episode in 2004, Alan thought the man was Ian Wooldridge, who had grown up in the New Forest and was just starting out on a career that would lead to his becoming one of the most highly regarded sports writers of his generation. For many years he was the chief sports correspondent of the *Daily Mail*.

To Alan's horror the result of this conversation was that, for two successive days, his life crisis was all across the top of page eight of the *Daily Mail*, the leading subject in its 'Paul Tanfield' gossip column. First it was:

NO-MORE-ROCK BATSMAN SAYS: 'IT'S AFRICA FOR ME'
Sheppard's friend to give up cricket for evangelism

Then the next day:

CRICKETING EVANGELIST'S WIFE TELLS HER STORY
We will not separate, says Mrs Rayment

The 1950s marked the rise of the celebrity gossip columns in Britain, with 'Paul Tanfield' of the *Daily Mail* competing for the best stories with the *Daily Express*'s 'William Hickey'. In May 1958, three months before the features on Alan, one of the 'Tanfield' team hit the jackpot when he spotted a young girl accompanying the rock'n'roller Jerry Lee Lewis at Heathrow airport. She was the 22-year-old singer's new wife, his third, and it turned out that not only was she his first cousin but she was only 13. That was not a page eight but a page one story.

The controversy generated by rock'n'roll sold newspapers, and Jerry Lee Lewis, whose 'Great Balls of Fire' had been number one in the hit parade in January, was its 'first wild man'. Brought up in a strict Baptist church in Louisiana, he has spent his life wrestling with the conflict between his religious faith and his love of what he calls 'the devil's music'. It is said that when he went into the studio to record 'Great Balls of Fire' he initially refused to sing. A tape survives of him arguing with the producer, asking "How can the devil save souls?"

By comparison Alan's story was mild fare, yet it was served up in a way that upset Alan for the rest of his life. In a handwritten page dated 2004, he wrote: 'Innovative writing by the young sports reporter teetered between fact and fanciful imagination, voiding the deep mysterious cause of a simple effect.' The 'simple effect' was that he was planning to give up both cricket and the ballroom, to follow in some way the calling of Christ.

Alan must have spoken of the possibility that he might coach that winter in South Africa. It was a common destination for professional cricketers, with many jobs available in the country's private schools. Did he go on to tell the journalist that he might stay in Africa and become a missionary – and, if so, was that just Alan thinking aloud, never dreaming the use that might be made of the remark? Or did the journalist add that detail to spice up the piece? Whatever the truth, the article always caused Alan to cringe. He had opened his heart to the young man, and it had all come out wrong.

'An ace rock'n'roller' with a glamorous wife, a friend of David Sheppard, giving up fame and fortune to be a missionary in Africa, it was just the stuff the paper's readers wanted, as his later note acknowledged:

> Religion? Money? Sex? All three! The *Daily Mail* grabbed the religion banana, served up 'missionary in Africa' and skidded away from the real story, which was much too deep for them.

Alan was wrestling with life-changing issues, and he was undoubtedly unwise to talk as he did to the reporter. According to the article he spoke to the reporter 'yesterday' in the pavilion at Bournemouth, 'waiting to bat for top-of-the-table Hampshire', which cannot be true as he had not been in the team for two months and the county were playing at Clacton. Nevertheless, the piece, by quoting him at length, does reveal something of his state of mind at that time.

> "I'm afraid I did not approve of what I saw on Saturday nights at our ballroom," Mr Rayment told me. "We had a bar, and that sort of thing. I came to realise that our clients, many of them little more than children, were being led away from God by our 'Rock'. After all, much of the music and lyrics are decadent.

"But I'm afraid my wife does not see things my way. At present she cannot understand my religious convictions. She is yet to be converted. It is all very difficult, and I can only pray. I have had long talks with David Sheppard, and he has given me wonderful advice.

"Now I must go wherever the Lord directs. At the moment I am not sure where that will be. But I hope to get a coaching job in South Africa this winter, so that I have plenty of time to study evangelism. Then I can become a missionary.

"I know my wife is agin' my plans. But I must do what the Lord tells me. That's why I'm leaving Hampshire. Who knows? – she may yet be converted."

Betty, predictably described as a '29-year-old brunette', was bewildered by the turn of events:

"I don't want to become an African missionary's wife. I want to stay with the school. I don't share my husband's views, and it's all rather awkward, particularly as it happened so suddenly. He's gone evangelical, undenominational and all that sort of thing."

The next day 'Tanfield' returned to Alan's story, starting this time with Betty, who revealed that Alan was not now planning to go to South Africa but to work alongside David Sheppard with London's poor:

The whole day long after my story appeared, her phone was ringing. "All over the place Christians have been praying for me and the children," said Betty. "I've just come back from a holiday in the Isle of Man, where I stayed at a hotel with some very wealthy Christian friends of Alan's. They were strictly teetotal, and all the time they were praying for my conversion. But I don't feel any change coming over me.

"What's wrong with people dancing, anyway?" she asked. "It's better for young people to work off their energy on the dance floor than to stand on street corners. Alan and I have had arguments about his beliefs. But we are not going to separate. And our three children will stay with us, wherever he goes."

Said Rayment, after putting his children to bed last night while his wife taught pupils at their dancing school, "All the boys and girls who go rock'n'rolling are not bad. But it's the way they dance and the music that often leads so many into trouble."

> Then he told me: "I haven't been given a job in South Africa and I don't know of one yet available in London, but I believe Christ will solve my problem. Betty, of course, is being materially practicable in wondering how we're going to feed and clothe the kids. But our problem will work out. She'll see."

In the event Alan went neither to South Africa nor to London that winter. Though in later life he came once more to appreciate the energy and skills of rock'n'roll dancing, he and Betty closed the ballroom and gave up their exhibitions. With money short, they removed the children from fee-paying schools, and they sold house, furniture and car.

A Christian friend Oliver Stott, a director of Dibben builders' merchants, rented them a semi-detached Victorian house in Belmont Road for two pounds a week and employed Alan for the winter, selling Aga cookers. He attended an American-style sales course, then drove around the Hampshire countryside in a company car, a Ford Prefect: "one of those long sausage-like things".

In the midst of a credit squeeze, Alan had little success with the Agas – "My heart wasn't really in it; I think I sold half a dozen in five months" – but till the end of March he also had a weekly wage of £7–15s a week from Hampshire. It was a great upheaval, but the family got by.

14

A summer at Lord's
1959

Alan had made an outstanding impression when he attended the MCC's Advanced Coaching Course at Lilleshall. He was a natural teacher, able not only to observe and analyse movement but to convey enthusiasm. Furthermore, when a coaching film was made, he was among those chosen to demonstrate the skills of the game.

> Peter May did the batting, Ray Smith of Essex the bowling, Godfrey Evans the wicket-keeping, Peter Sainsbury the close catching and me the fielding.
>
> The bigwigs at Lord's were aghast with the film of Peter May because he didn't pick his bat up straight. But so many players didn't. Clyde Walcott used to pick his up towards point.
>
> My bit was to run in from cover, pick up the ball and throw it in. Harry Altham was perturbed because I didn't throw it from lowdown, the Australian way. But someone told me that Harold Abrahams, the athletics commentator, had seen the film, and he'd said what a wonderful javelin throw I had, with so much power.

A job coaching cricket in a school was an obvious way forward for Alan, and he was offered one at the Royal Masonic School in Hertfordshire, an institution that catered for the children of Freemasons. Alan, with some hesitation, had become a Mason two years earlier, but in his new state of mind neither the freemasonry nor the coaching job had any appeal to him.

> I remember typing a letter of resignation from the Masonic Lodge. When I got going on a typewriter, I would be buzzing. I sent them a four-page theological treatise blasting the nonsense of Fremasonry.
>
> And I didn't want to go and coach in a public school. To me, that was like putting an old racehorse out to grass. I was in the midst of an intellectual awakening, a renaissance of the mind. I had a great thirst for knowledge. I wanted to do something creative, something dynamic, not fade away as a cricket coach in a school. At that stage

> I thought I was called to go into the church. Therefore I should go to theological college. But there were other things to sort out first.

Alan's very public religious conversion had changed not only his inner life but the responses he got from other people.

> I'd always been a very sociable person, but it was different now. It had been in the press that I'd got religion – all that newspaper crap. So now people were wary of me. I guess it was a natural reaction, but there were people who treated me as if I'd got horns coming out of my head, had grown bigger ears or turned green.

One person who proved a good listener was Harry Altham, Hampshire President, MCC Treasurer and retired Winchester College schoolmaster.

> To some people Harry Altham might have seemed stuffy but never to me. He was the best type of old-fashioned schoolmaster – and the most helpful counsellor I had on my marriage. He had empathy, a listening air and always a few words of wisdom.
>
> One day he said to me, "Would you like to come to Lord's for the summer as one of the staff coaches?" There was a vacancy, and at that point it was the only sensible thing on offer.

Back in 1945, as an eager sixteen-year-old, Alan had attended MCC's Easter coaching classes and been inspired by Frank Lee. Now, as his first assignment at Lord's, he was to be 'Frank Lee' to another generation of youngsters in the Easter classes. He was allocated to a net of boys, among whom was a 15-year-old Marlburian, Michael Griffith, who was the son of MCC's Assistant Secretary, Billy Griffith. It was an indication, though Alan did not realise it, that the powers at Lord's had high expectations of him.

Initially, till he had an 'unfortunate row' with his father, Alan stayed with his parents in Finchley, travelling home to Southampton on Saturday evening and returning first thing on Monday. He was worshipping at All Souls Church in Langham Place, where the rector John Stott was a leading figure in the evangelical movement. Among the church wardens was George Cansdale, a former superintendant of London Zoo and now a familiar figure on television, presenting animal programmes. Hearing of his predicament, Cansdale invited Alan to lodge with him and his wife at their home in Lyndale Avenue, off the bottom of Hendon Way.

> "Come down the garden with me, old chap," he said on my first night there. "I want to show you one or two things." His secretary

came with us and, while he was chatting, she dived into a cage, then said to me, "Alan, would you like to hold this a minute?" I turned round, and she dumped this great python on me.

They were good fun.

Head Coach at Lord's was Bill Watkins, who had been on the Middlesex staff in the 1930s without ever establishing himself in the county's first-choice side. Born in Ealing in 1904, he had been at Lord's most of his adult life and was a devoted servant of MCC.

> He was a small Cockney sparrow, a lovely man, a real professional of the old school, married to Lord's. If he were in the army, he might become a corporal, but he wouldn't quite make a sergeant-major.

Watkins had three other assistants: Len Muncer of Middlesex and Glamorgan (who had bowled Alan 'through the gate' when Alan made his Hampshire debut in 1949), Harry Sharp of Middlesex and Bill Morris of Essex, all men happy to give their lives to the game. Their primary responsibility was to a group of some 15 or 20 youngsters who were on the ground staff that summer, coaching them in the nets in the hope that they might become professional cricketers. In the old-fashioned ways of MCC the youngsters had to be available to bowl to any member of the club who requested a net.

MCC ran a full programme of out-matches, taking teams of members to play at all the top schools, and the coaches were often brought in to add their professional skills to the sides. Alan played in a number of these games, scoring centuries at Lancing and Ampleforth.

> I did score quite a few runs that season. In the MCC averages I finished very high, fifth or sixth. Len Hutton, I remember, was top.

Len Muncer, Harry Sharp and Alan were all in a side that played at Eton where, despite having five Test cricketers in their side including the Australians Ben Barnett and Keith Miller, they lost to the school side. Alan top-scored with 48, leaving this brief note on the game:

> Played at Eton under captaincy of RWV Robins. Keith Miller, on instructions from RWV, bowled a very fast lifter at a 16-year-old playing his first game for Eton. The boy did not see the ball as it whizzed under his chin. Ben Barnett, keeping wicket, had to jump high to catch the ball. Keith followed through and thumped the white-faced kid on the shoulder, saying "Get behind 'em, son." AWH at mid-off heard and saw it all.

MCC v Australian Old Collegians, Lord's, June 1959
back: Alan Rayment, Colin Drybrough, Gerry Wilson, John Mortimore, David Eames, Don Bennett; front: George Tribe, Billy Griffith, David Sheppard (captain), Gamini Goonesena, Jack Manning

Alan hit 77 and 44 in a two-day match against Club Cricket Conference: "Billy Griffith came up to me after my 44. 'Thank you, Alan,' he said, 'for that most entertaining innings.'" Alan also opened the batting with David Sheppard in a game against the Australian Old Collegians.

His main work, however, was with the youngsters on the ground staff, and he grew increasingly frustrated by what he witnessed.

> The boys enjoyed it, but there was not a lot of talent there. Very few, if any, of them were going to make a county staff so why had they been taken on? Who was doing the selecting? If they were apprentices in a trade and played club cricket, wouldn't it be better for them? The coaching was all based on playing pretty shots so they didn't score many runs in the out-matches. And the system of bowling to the members in the nets, it was so archaic. Why couldn't the members bowl to themselves?

Alan's mind was full of the books he was reading: the radical Methodist theologian Leslie Weatherhead, the Swiss psychoanalyst Carl Jung and the Jesuit Pierre Teilhard de Chardin, who sought to fuse the scientific theory of evolution with a less literal interpretation of the Bible. At the same time he was alive to the world around him, questioning so much of what he saw.

> I was quite left-wing in my thinking. I was interested in change, and I could be quite outspoken if I saw injustice. That's why I became a community worker. I have an analytical ability and a boldness to attack. But I wasn't specifically political. I was asked once by the Liberal Party in Southampton to stand in an election. I said to them, "I am very honoured to be asked, but I just could not lie as much as I would have to do."

It all came to a head one day in early August. Each of the coaches had a group of boys in a net, with Alan in the next net to Bill Watkins.

> This boy in Bill's net picked up a half-volley outside off stump, on the up, and he hit an on-drive into the sky towards the mower sheds a long, long way away. 'Gee,' I thought. 'That's a great shot.'
>
> Then I saw Bill Watkins going down the net, wagging his finger at this boy, remonstrating with him, demonstrating that he should have pushed the ball down the line to mid-off. I thought, 'What the hell are you doing?' I was so incensed by it.
>
> I said to my crew, "Get as many balls as you can." I found a box and some gloves, and I went into the net. The coaches didn't normally bat so there was quite a stir, and I hit every ball as far as I could. I was playing flat-bat tennis shots over the bowler's heads, everything. There were balls all over the Nursery Ground. "Hit the bloody thing," I kept shouting. There was quite a buzz among the boys.
>
> When the session finished, we were walking behind the Grand Stand, and this boy came up to me. A fair-haired lad, quite a good off-spinner. He said, "What was all that about?" I said, "This game is not about looking pretty. It's about scoring runs. Putting some beef and timing into it, not just making a good impression on a coach."

What happened next is not entirely clear. In his notes for this book Alan said that he complained in writing to Billy Griffith about 'the whole ethos of the ground staff boys' but, in talking to me, there was no mention of this letter of complaint.

The day after the incident in nets I was playing in an out-match. Then the following day, about half past ten in the morning, one of the stewards came down. He said, "Mr Griffith and Mr Altham would like to see you in Mr Griffith's office." It was like being called to the headmaster's study. 'Uh-uh,' I thought. 'I've got the sack, for causing a stir.'

When I entered the room, they asked me to sit down, and the manner of their greeting was friendlier than I expected.

"Well, Alan," Harry Altham said. "I understand that you have some thoughts about the ground staff and the type of coaching that we give to them. We'd like you to tell us what you think about your experience here."

Harry Altham

From that I got the feeling that I wasn't in really serious trouble. In any case I wasn't a kid anymore, I'd run a successful business dealing with the public, and I was happy to say what I thought. So I did not hold back.

I started by saying that the way the boys were recruited and the purposes for which they were recruited were out of date. "There are a few who have potential but maybe only two or three." I questioned why they had to bowl to members; I said it was the old pro-am divide, and I didn't agree with that. Harry knew me well enough. He knew where I was coming from.

Then I criticised the coaching. "These boys, when they go to play out-matches, they look pretty but they don't hit the bloody ball." I told them about the incident in the net and Bill Watkins' wagging finger. "That to me is all wrong," I said.

When I finished, Billy Griffith spoke. "Well, we have been informed about your views and about what happened in the nets, and we have been discussing the matter with the members of the committee. It has been decided to offer you the post of Head Coach from next season."

> This was a complete shock. I was silent for what seemed like a long time; it might have been 30 seconds, it might have been a minute and a half. I was thinking like mad: 'Wow! This is Lord's, a place I love. So much started for me here. And they are offering me this wonderful job.'

It was an extraordinary moment, not only in Alan's life but in the history of MCC's coaching scheme. And it was a great tribute to the vision and humanity of Harry Altham, that he saw the potential to revolutionise the outdated ways of Lord's and, I suspect, to provide Alan with the sense of life-direction that he had lost in the turmoil of his past two years.

> I thought and thought, and in the long pause I came to two conclusions. One, that I couldn't possibly take Bill Watkins' job; Lord's had been his life since he was a boy. And two, I had no real inner desire to be a cricket coach; I wanted to go to theological college or university.

If Alan had thrown himself into the job, as he had done with his dance teaching, I have no doubt that he would have been an inspirational figure, a great force for good in the world of cricket. Even in old age he was still passionate about the best way to develop the talents of the young.

> Coaches talk far too much. I was watching a net recently, and this coach said something nearly every ball. It wasn't about the pupil; it was about the ego of the coach. What was it John Wayne said to Clint Eastwood? "A little tip for you. Talk low, talk slow, and don't say too much." I think Clint Eastwood took that on, didn't he?
>
> You can have too many coaches. When more and more are appointed, there comes to be a safety in everything being orthodox and correct. Coaching is not about that. It's about encouragement, enabling, about fun and enthusiasm – because cricket is a game. You're not doing a PhD in Molecular Science. It's a game.

Eventually Alan replied to Billy Griffith's offer. He expressed his concern for the future of Bill Watkins, and he explained that he did not want to stay in cricket as a coach. "Therefore," he said, "the obvious conclusion is that I must resign from my position. I will let you have my letter tomorrow." And with that he returned to Southampton, to Betty and the three children – with a fourth on the way. His future remained far from clear.

*

During his summer at Lord's Alan was persuaded by Betty to take to the dance floor one more time. The request came from a Miss Crystal Holme, the principal and owner of Prince's Mead, a preparatory day school for girls in Edgar Road, Winchester.

> Miss Holme asked Betty if we would give a ballroom dancing exhibition for a parents' evening. At first I refused, I did not want to return to dancing, but I gave in after I had met Miss Holme at Prince's Mead. She was an Oxford graduate and ran a 'posh' school.
>
> I borrowed a tailsuit, and we performed in a wooden school hut. With tables down each side it was long and narrow and, with Betty's big dress spinning out, we knocked over one or two bottles and glasses, but the exhibition went down very well.

Betty formed a friendship with Crystal Holme and, when Alan returned from Lord's, the headmistress was quick to offer a solution to his lack of income. "Alan must come and do some decorating for me," she said.

> So three or four days after coming down from Lord's I was off up to Winchester, stripping wallpaper from the high Victorian ceiling of her sitting room. Having a whale of a time. Earning more money than I was at Lord's, without the expenses. I was still there at the start of the term.
>
> I was hanging wallpaper on the ceiling one day when Crystal came in. "Take off your overalls, please, Alan, and put on a sports jacket," she said. "We need you to look after the kindergarten boys."
> One of the teachers had gone into hospital with tonsillitis.

Alan was put in charge of a group of seven small boys. Then, when his teaching ability became clear, he was given responsibility for a class of 14 ten-year-old girls, teaching English, History, Geography, Scripture and Games. He stayed with them for eighteen months.

> I was the only master, with my own staff room in the attic. Cook used to bring up my lunch on a tray.
>
> I was put in charge of the senior netball team. I used to play with them; the games were a bit rough at times. Matron complained to Miss Holme: "Mr Rayment is sending gals up with bleeding knees." They became the best netball team in Winchester, and we won the athletics, too.

"Of course you must play some cricket," Crystal Holme told Alan in the summer term of 1960, and he was granted leave to appear four times for Hampshire in the 2nd XI Championship, captaining the team and nurturing such young players as Alan Castell, Alan Wassell and the Antiguan Danny Livingstone.

> I enjoyed my time at Prince's Mead. I thought about training to be a teacher at King Alfred College, but I wouldn't have had enough money to support the family.
>
> I'm a Double Gemini; we're versatile. I always wanted to do something more challenging, something I hadn't already done.

With a large family to support, his next venture was to set up an estate agency, working from an office at home. But the story of that episode was to be told in the unwritten volume three of this autobiography.

*

At some point on his life's journey Alan wrote a poem, addressed to God, called 'Happiness'. It has nine verses, of which these are four:

> Happiness is learning
> a little bit each day,
> young or old still yearning
> for adventure on life's way.
>
> Happiness is loving
> a little more each day,
> list'ning, caring, sharing,
> affirming you always.
>
> ......
>
> Happiness is laughing
> at myself, with you,
> at life's crazy paving –
> let's dance and not be blue.
>
> Through learning, growing, knowing,
> giving, loving true; thru'
> the humbling pain of living,
> may 'IT' shine – through me, through you ...
> HAPPINESS!

15

Later life

In October 1993, at the age of 65, Alan typed out a formal Curriculum Vitae, listing his qualifications, career and recreational interests. His summary of his career after 1961, when he left Prince's Mead School, reads as follows:

1961-65 **PROPRIETOR** of ALAN RAYMENT & CO, Estate Agents in Southampton. Pioneering a very successful business in residential and land sales, employing a staff of six. Sold in 1965 due to ambition to serve the Church in an ordained or lay capacity.

1965 **CANDIDATE** for ordination in the Church of England. Considered too radical and marriage, at that stage, not sufficiently stable.

1965-67 **SELF EMPLOYED** in new Double Glazing business (franchise). Successful until franchiser and supplier filed for bankruptcy. Thereafter, until going to college, several fill-in jobs in which low motivation and depression were experienced but needs of family maintained.

1967-69 **STUDENT** at Westhill College of Education, studying full-time for University of Birmingham 'Certificate in Community Work'. Absence from home in Hampshire the catalyst for divorce, loss of six children and home.

1969-70 **ASSISTANT WARDEN**, Abbey Community Centre, Westminster, London. Responsible for group bookings, catering and promotion of new welfare and voluntary service groups.

1970-71 **SELF EMPLOYED**: PROPERTY RENOVATION BUSINESS in Canning Town, East London at the beginning of second marriage to a headteacher and unable to obtain employment as a community worker due to Local Government reorganisation following the Seebohm Report.

1971-74 **WARDEN**: PIONEERING THE NEW POLLARDS HILL COMMUNITY CENTRE for London Borough of Merton Education Department. Leading the promotion of a new Community Association and developing 60 new groups to meet a variety of community needs in education, social welfare and recreation.

1974-78 **SENIOR COMMUNITY WORKER** with West Sussex County Council based at Haywards Heath. Pioneering community work in combined rural and London commuter belt area: identifying needs and resources, using a catalytic approach in promoting educational and volunteer projects; self-help and support groups; public relations and fund raising; liaison and negotiations with civic authorities and business groups; public speaking engagements. Field Work Supervisor for post-graduate students, University of Sussex. Occasional private counselling work.

1978-80 **POST GRADUATE STUDENT**. University of Sussex Masters Degree course in Social Work. Occasional private counselling work.

1980-82 **SENIOR SOCIAL WORKER** with West Sussex County Council. Family crisis oriented caseload; foster and adoptive parent vetting and counselling; court work and public speaking engagements.

1982-86 **SELF EMPLOYED PSYCHOTHERAPIST AND PROPERTY CONSULTANT**. Living in Sussex and, following divorce, in Hampshire, a period of transition towards a lifestyle of worldwide travel, new experiences and working on autobiographical material from journals. **COMMENT**: From 1983 to 1993 I have been living IT rather than writing IT.

1987-91 **RESIDENT IN CALIFORNIA AND HAWAII** and visits to AUSTRALIA, to broaden cultural, ethnological and spiritual experience, gathering material for writing on a variety of subjects. Renovated property in Malibu: set up a Real Estate Company negotiating hotel resort and golf course properties in Hawaii, California and NSW Australia. Failed to close deals before recession affected market; in debt; closed business. Co-wrote plot and outline of a screenplay the development of which by a third writer became verbose and unsaleable, though registered in USA. Returned to England penniless.

1991-93 **TRANSITION COUNSELLOR.** Giving assistance to family and friends through personal crises, career change, moving house, and growth in awareness and spirituality. (Not paid.) At the same time studying metaphysics, writing and seeking to clarify my own near future. Conclusion: Continue to study and learn; research and prepare autobiography and other books/articles ... and plan further travel experience.

An album contains several newspaper profiles of Alan during his years as a community worker. In one, published in 1972, he was warden of the Pollards Hill Community Centre in an area of Mitcham where new housing had led to a great change in the local population.

> "You have got to remember," Alan Rayment said, "that a community spirit is not something which happens overnight. It takes years before you can begin to see it growing."
>
> Before the upheavals in the area there was a good community spirit. Now many have died or moved away. Newcomers have taken their place both in the council houses and the rows of privately owned semis. "Given time and patience that same spirit of belonging will come back," he promised.
>
> Occasionally, as he sits in his office and thinks of the vast blocks of flats stretching towards Mitcham Common, the many closes and groves towards Manor-way, and the honeycombs of brand new houses, he feels like a man trying to melt the tip of an iceberg with a lighted match.

His work had much in common with that of a local vicar, only without the religion and with more emphasis on having a good time.

> The law requires that he is in the building during hours when it is used at night for dances. This he regards not as an imposition but as a chance to meet more people.

Three years later he was featured several times in the *Mid Sussex Times*: launching a newspaper for the blind, developing a holiday play scheme for primary-age children and being celebrated as one of a pair of council employees who 'somehow manage to combine a day-to-day job with a genuine interest in people'.

> These two people ... make me wonder if bureaucracy is not going full circle and we are going back to a situation where humans really care about one another.

Also in the album is a testimonial from the Deputy Director of Social Services, mentioning Alan's participation in the department's cricket matches:

> He performed at a level far above his team mates yet in every way he was a team man, accepting instructions from the captain and working wholeheartedly for the side, giving great support and encouragement to everyone.

*The Mid Sussex Social Services Department team in 1976
(Alan, though he played, is not in the photograph)*

This testimonial was one of three written for Alan in September 1986, at a time when he was once more embarking on a new journey, away from the world of community work. Another was from the chairman of a property company whose retirement from the business Alan had negotiated.

> I highly recommend Mr Rayment as a patient but tough negotiator, able to draw on his many skills and deep experience in business, life and interpersonal relationships. He is a man of the very highest integrity with qualities of drive and leadership, who is such a positive thinker that he is able to overcome many and varied problems when he is fighting for any cause in which he believes.

The third testimonial was from Colin Ingleby-Mackenzie:

> I played both with him and also captained him and throughout my playing days he was the most excellent team man ... I have also met him on a number of occasions since our combined retirements and he has shown both business expertise and enthusiasm in everything he does. He has great ability and insight into people's characters and

has a number of qualities which are unusual in the normal first-class cricketer. I have no hesitation in writing a letter of support for him in any particular new career that he chooses.

The trigger for this change of direction had occurred three years earlier, an episode in his life which he part-described in an unfinished piece of writing.

His second marriage to Joan had entered challenging territory where, in Alan's words, 'We were intellectually and emotionally involved in a tug-o-war between loyalty to each other – and to our Christian marriage vows – versus a rumbling inner volcano of energies threatening to burst our constraining defences and erupt into a flowing freedom to explore Life.'

At the end of a holiday in Cornwall Joan travelled to London to spend time with her recently bereaved father and to meet up with old friends from her days at the Mayflower Centre where, through Grace and David Sheppard, she had been introduced to Alan. Meanwhile Alan booked into a hotel on the Isle of Wight for a four-day retreat, to read works of theology and to think about his life. It turned out that the hotel, Holmes Court in Colwell Bay, was up for sale, and he started to hatch a plan. If he could raise the funds, he would purchase the hotel and create a conference and counselling centre.

> I envisaged a community with a non-religious ethos but open to individual exploration of untapped creative and spiritual resources and healing of psychological problems.

After going home to Sussex, he returned to the hotel for a longer stay. He packed a dozen books, including 'Someday I'll Find You', the recently published autobiography of Harry Williams, an Anglican priest who was sceptical about much of conventional Christianity.

> The book, packed with details of his often agonising search for faith in God uncluttered by religion, provided evidence of mystical experiences similar to my own and theological criticism that caused me, metaphorically, to shout from the rooftops, 'Yes, Yes, YES!!'

Alan was in a state of heightened sensitivity when he sat in his room on the first evening. He opened his bible at random and read words from the second chapter of Habakkuk:

> And the Lord answered me: "Write the vision; make it plain upon tablets, so that he may run who reads it. For still the vision awaits its time; it hastens to the end – it will not lie. If it seems slow, wait for it; it will surely come, it will not delay."

Alan wrote out his vision of the conference and counselling centre.

> But I felt I was pushing my ideas against a gentle flow of 'other' energy that slowly, slowly filled me and enveloped me.
>
> For an indeterminate period of time my whole being was on a different plane of existence. My mind was burgeoning with knowledge and understanding and, as in the three exceptional encounters with the Divine Presence in 1957 and 1958, I was filled with 'the peace of God which passeth all understanding'.

The following morning he woke in the same state of peacefulness but also with a renewed awareness that orthodox religion was not providing him with the answers he needed:

> that my personal twenty-five year debate about inconsistencies in Christian theology in general, and in particular regarding Christ-centred mystical experiences that I and many thousands of people had witnessed in many publications over hundreds of years, …

Here in mid-sentence the fragment of recollection ends.

The experience in the hotel was the trigger for another upheaval in his life, one that saw him travel abroad in his search for greater spiritual understanding. In April 1987, in a further fragment, he was on a beach in Malibu, watching with admiration the healthy energy of the young surfers, yet alienated from the 'humdrum acquisitiveness' that underpinned their world. He was tempted to rejoin 'that energetic world of business or community creativity', with offers from friends to engage in 'international real estate', yet another part of him wanted to withdraw from it, to write an autobiography, to make sense of his life's experiences.

> Here am I, alone, caught between earth and heaven – the daring edge of choice – the challenge and risk of change. Choice between the worldly multi career driven – the work at anything to earn a crust habit I had experienced thus far on my journey – or to countenance the more esoteric, artistic and lonely endeavour to write a book … or two or more?

Perhaps the choice was made for him when in 1991 a property deal in Australia fell through, the result of a recession, and he returned to England penniless. Living on a state pension, he settled to the writing of a three-volume autobiography. A handwritten fragment, dated April 2003, reflects on his motive for this writing:

TO SHARE – to share the journey of one man who has been blessed with other than average spiritual experiences. From those timeless moments of November 5th 1957 ... those moments and others later of BEING ONE – of the ONENESS OF 'LOVE DIVINE, ALL LOVES EXCELLING'.

For short and long periods I have temporarily forgotten, drifted towards worldliness or momentarily rebelled because of the seeming improbability of surviving without compromising totally with consumer-driven materialism etc etc.

Compromise is necessary. Balance is vital!!

The previous day he had been 'blessed with a beautiful and encouraging message': "ENJOY BECOMING A GOOD WRITER". Unquestionably Alan did find joy in the writing and, although there were times when he felt overwhelmed by the scale of the autobiographical task he had set himself, he remained engaged with it to the end of his days.

He never did discover a religious community in which he felt entirely at home. He had been scarred by the tone of those *Daily Mail* articles, and he saved discussion of religion for those who wanted to know. Even in his obituary in the magazine *The Cricketer*, there was a hint of treating him as a crank, and he would have hated that. He tried always to keep a balance between the spiritual and the worldly.

The game of cricket had been his first love, in those early years on Arden Field; it opened so many doors for him and gave him so much life experience. So there was a special joy in the way, after his journey through life, he returned to that world in his last years. At Hampshire Old Players' Reunions, the Dorset Cricket Society and the Hambledon Dining Club, he became a familiar and much-loved figure, always radiating positive energy.

He received much loving support from Elizabeth, his companion in his last years, and there were many memorable days out. Tour de force was the 90th birthday party in May 2018 when, thinking he was stopping for a quick lunchtime sandwich, he found himself surrounded by a roomful of his cricketing friends.

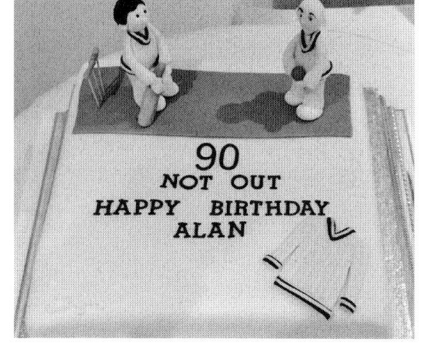

A chance reunion at Cheltenham in 2018: Alan and Elizabeth (right) with Brian Wilde, fellow Community Work student in the 1960s, and his wife Ann

The following May he went for the last time to the Isle of Wight, scene of happy childhood holidays and always a place close to his heart. Complete with hamper, Elizabeth drove him across the ferry to the new ground at Newclose, south of Newport, where Hampshire were playing their first match on the island since 1962. In glorious sunshine he watched with admiration as Sam Northeast and Ajinkya Rahane stroked cultured centuries, and he was on sparkling form when interviewed during Radio Solent's ball-by-ball commentary. Sixty-six years earlier Alan had scored a fifty for Hampshire at the opening of the ground at Cowes and, as the last survivor of that team of the early 1950s, there was a magic about his presence that day.

He joined a fitness class on his local beach, not embarrassed to be the only man in a group of elderly ladies, but in his 92nd year his physical problems began to mount, curtailing his trips out of the flat. Despite this, his telephone conversations with friends remained uplifting.

He had, as Colin Ingleby-Mackenzie wrote, 'a number of qualities which are unusual in the normal first-class cricketer', and those qualities made him a 'character' in the best sense of the word. Though he explored his past with meticulous energy in his writing, he remained alive to new ideas, always knowing that there was more to life than he would ever understand.

He never finished this book nor started Volume Three, and there is some sadness in that. Yet I find it hard to be sad when I think of Alan. He exuded such a joy of life.

INDEX *(for reasons of space, Alan's close family members are omitted)*

A
Abrahams, Harold 173
Aird, Ronnie 23
Allen, Dave 6,8,16,18
Allen, Gubby 22,25-7,60,78
Altham, Harry 59,117,129, 173-4,178-9
Ann (dance teacher) 138,151-2
Appleyard, Bob 102
Arlott, John 59,66,87-8,96,120
Arnold, Johnny 35-6,48-9, 55-6,73-4,78-9,84-5,90
Arnold, WJ 97-8
Astaire, Fred 12,32
Attenborough, David 10
Attlee, Clement 57

B
Bailey, Jim 35-6,42-51,73, 83,106-8,111,115
Barclay, John 15,144
Barnard, Mike 16,37, 129-30,150,167-9
Barnes, Alison 6
Barnett, Ben 175
Bedford, Ian 23,76
Bedser, Alec 42,78,84-5
Begin, Menachem 144
Benaud, Richie 122
Bennett, Don 176
Benson, Ivy 136
Biles, Joan 64
Biles, Timothy 6-8,18,61-4
Binney, Colonel 82
Blake, David 37,75,79
Bligh, Ivo 77
Bolt, Usain 84
Botham, Ian 13
Bowyer, Basil 64
Bradman, Don 42,63-4
Bradstock, andrew 6
Bridger, John 37,75,79,86
Brown, Freddie 60
Brown, George 106

Brown, Syd 77
Burden, Mervyn 117,126-7,129,168
Burke, Mrs 65
Buse, Bertie 17,120

C
Cannings, Vic 73,75-7,83, 92,101-2,116,119, 126-7,142-6,148,167
Cansdale, George 174-5
Cartridge, Don 116-7
Cartwright, Tom 13,162
Carty, Dick 37,76,94
Castell, Alan 181
Chester, Frank 60,90
Chester, Rex 69-71
Chester, Rex jnr 70-1
Clark, Ron 90-1
Clarke, Kenny 135
Coldwell, Len 167
Collingwood, Paul 145
Compton, Denis 7,25,40, 60,68,77-8,86,124
Compton, Leslie 124
Conan Doyle, Arthur 107-11,114-5
Constantine, Learie 22,40,83
Cook, Sam 86-8
Cottam, Bob 84
Couper, Michael 156
Cowdrey, Colin 26,102
Coxon, Alec 86
Cramphorn, Iris 21

D
Dare, Reg 27,37,97,101, 116-7,119,146
David (ballroom manager) 138,151-2
Dawson, Gilbert 35,73
Dawson, Harold 37
Dean, Tom 37,49
Dear, Mr & Mrs 33

Debnam, Alec 75,77,87,94,97-8
de Chardin, Teilhard 177
Dewes, John 77-8
Dewhurst, Tommy 27
Dexter, Ted 146
Dodds, Dickie 148
Doggart, Hubert 77
Donnelly, Martin 55-6
Drake, Norman 168
Drybrough, Colin 176

E
Eagar, Desmond 28-9,31-2,35-8,40-4, 48,51-4,56,59,62,65-6, 69,73-5,77,79,85,87,98, 101-2,117,119-20,122-3, 127-9,132,142,146,169
Eames, David 176
Eastwood, Clint 179
Edrich, Bill 77,124
Emmett, George 87
Evans, Godfrey 78,100,148-9,173

F
Federer, Roger 83
Ferguson, Bill 63
Fitzgerald, Michael 23
Flavell, Jack 127,167
Flintoff, Andrew 12
Fowler, Archie 20,23
Fred (gardener) 152
Fry, CB 21

G
Garland, Judy 32
Gimblett, Harold 42,48-9,53-4,114,120
Goddard, Tom 86-8
Gold, Harry 49-50
Goonesena, Gamini 176
Gough, Darren 12

Gover, Alf 42,70
Gower, David 13,84
Grace, WG 110
Graham, Billy 161
Graveney, Tom 83
Gray, Jimmy 12,35,37-8,43,
58,74-6,84,86-7,89,96-7,
100-1,116,119,122,125,
127-9,141-2,150,168-9
Gray, Laurie 23-4
Griffith, Billy 143,174,176-9
Griffith, Michael 174
Guard, David 37,40-1,43,48

H

Hadlee, Richard 55
Hadlee, Walter 55-6
Hammond, Wally 22
Harris, Charlie 44-6,48,59,
100-1,145,148
Harrison, Leo 36-7,75,
83-4,87,94,96-7,100-1,
116-7,119-20,128-9,168-9
Harvey, Cyril 28
Harvey, Neil 122
Hassett, Lindsay 22,144
Heath, George 35,41,43,73
Heath, Malcolm 35,37,61,
129-30,132-3,166,168
Helpmann, Robert 31
Hendren, Dennis 42
Hendren, Patsy
25,28,35,40,42,156
Herman, Lofty 35-6,73
Hill, Eric 48-9
Hill, Ernest 106,110
Hill, Gerry 7,35,38,41,43,
47-8,50,68,74-5,79,86,101-2,
106-8,110-1,116,119,123
Hills, Joe 107-8
Hobbs, Jack 21
Holme, Crystal 180-1
Holmes, Bob 33,58,65,91
Holt, Arthur 1-2,35-6,38,
53-4,59,64,75-6,83,94,97-8,
102,116-7,129,145,149,168

Horton, Henry 12,75,122,
127-8,141,150,168-9
Hulme, Gilly 136
Hulme, Joe 21-2,72,120
Hunt, Mrs 71,92,104-5
Hurst, Ken 70-1,90-1
Hutton, Len 42,78,125,175

I

Illingworth, Ray 125
Ingleby-Mackenzie, Colin
129,132-3,146,
166-9,185-6,189
Ivy (housekeeper)
140,150-2,159-60

J

Jacques, Henry 130
Jessop, Gilbert 77-8
Jesty, Trevor 84
Johnston, Bill 146
Jung, Carl 177

K

Karinthy, Frigyes 106
Keeton, Wally 44-5
Kelly, Gene 12
Kennedy, Alex 106
Knights, Ernie 43
Knott, Charlie
35-6,43-4,46-9,52,74,
79,86-7,98,101-2,105

L

Laker, Jim 42,147
Lambert, George 87-8
Langridge, Jim 102
Langridge, John 42
Leach, Ralph 114
Leadbeater, Eddie 86,102
Lee, Frank
19-21,28,40,42,79,174
Lewis, CS 156-7
Lewis, Denise 84
Lewis, Jerry Lee 169-70
Lindwall, Ray 84

Livingstone, Danny 181
Lloyd, Elizabeth
6,10,15,18,188-9
Lock, Tony 123
Locke, Colonel 91
Lorimer, Malcolm 6
Luckes, Wally 108

M

McCall, Ken 106,114-5
McCanlis, Ken 80
McCarthy, Cuan 102
McCorkell, Neil 35,37,43-4,
48,52-3,56,73,79,82-3,87,
94,96-7,100-2,106-8,111,118
McIndoe, David 143
McIntyre, Arthur 42
McMahon, Jack 128
Maharajah of Porbandar 111
Manning, Jack 176
Marlar, Robin 126
Marshall, Roy
12,82,84,117,121-2,
125,127,129,141,167-9
May, Peter 77-8,147,173
Mead, Philip 106
Meads, Eric 45
Meyer, Jack 107-8,111-4
Miller, Keith 22,175
Milton, Arthur 38
Mobey, George 17
Monroe, Marilyn 12
Morris, Bill 175
Mortimore, John 77,176
Muncer, Len 41,175
Murphy, E 23

N

Navratilova, Martina 83
Northeast, Sam 189

O

Oakley-John, Alan 161-2
Oakman, Alan 127
O'Connor, Jack 143
Osborne, Bert 137

O'Shea, D 23

P
Panesar, Monty 12
Paris, Cecil 74,98
Parkhouse, Gilbert 41
Pearce, WK 27-8,31
Pearson, Derek 167
Perks, Reg 101
Pietersen, Kevin 12
Pitman, Ray 117,168-9
Pothecary, Sam 60,83
Prince Philip 59-60,146-7
Pritchard, Tom 76
Prouton, Ralph 37,116-7

Q
HM Queen Elizabeth II 146-7

R
Rahane, Ajinkya 189
Rait Kerr, Colonel 20
Ramadhin, Sonny 81-2,84
Ramprakash, Mark 12
Ransitsinhji, KS 77
Ransom, Vic 37,43,48,79
Ratcliffe, Alan 23
Richard of Kent, Prince 143
Richardson, Peter 122
Rimmel, Tony 80
Robertson, Jack 42,77
Robins, Walter 20,22-4,60,78,175
Rogers, Neville 35-6,43,49,73,82,84,86-7,94,100-1,116,128-9,169
Ronaldo, Cristiano 83
Root, Joe 74
Ross, Edmundo 136
Rowe, Arthur 72

S
Sainsbury, Peter 125-7,129-30,132,148,159,162,168,173
Samuel, Leith 161-2

Sandham, Andrew 42
Scantlebury, Margaret 165
Scantlebury, Raymond 162,165-6
Shackleton, Derek 12,36-7,41,44,49,51,54,56,58,73,75-7,83-5,94,101-2,116-7,119,122-3,125,128,132,145,166-8
Shackleton, Kathy 84
Sharp, Harry 175
Shearer, Moira 31
Sheppard, David 6,77,80,146,156,158-62,165-6,170-1,176,186
Sheppard, Grace 80,158-60,165,186
Shirreff, Alan 31,38,78
Short, Peter 91
Silvester, Gwen 130,132
Silvester, Victor 130,136
Sime, Bill 44
Sims, Jim 23
Sinatra, Frank 120
Smith, Chris 84
Smith, Don 126
Smith, Mike 148
Smith, Ray 173
Sobers, Gary 84
Sprankling, Len 40,51,63,101
Stacey, John 23
Stewart, Micky 129
Stoop, Adrian 60
Stott, John 174
Stott, Oliver 172
Surridge, Stuart 129
Sutcliffe, Bert 55-6
Sutherland, Pete 21

T
Taylor, John 37
Tennyson, Lord 35,106
Thomson, Ian 127
Tom (Geordie) 163-5

Townsend, Alan 144
Tremlett, Maurice 119
Tribe, George 176
Trueman, Fred 12,86,102,166
Tulk, Derek 61

V
Valentine, Alf 82
Vaughan, Michael 12

W
Walcott, Clyde 82,173
Walford, Micky 106-8
Walker, Cliff 35-8,43,50,73-7,86-7,94,97,101,116,119,122,132
Walker, Marion 37
Wardle, Johnny 86,102
Warne, Shane 12-3
Warner, Pelham 20,22-3
Wassell, Alan 181
Watkins, Bill 175,177-9
Wayne, John 179
Weatherhead, Leslie 177
Webb, Elizabeth 71-2,92
Webb, Harold 71-2,92
Weekes, Everton 13,63,82-3,85
Wells, Bomber 11,13
White, Butch 84,168
Wignall, Bill 23
Wilde, Ann 189
Wilde, Brian 189
Williams, Harry 186
Wilson, Gerry 176
Woodcock, John 15
Woodhead, Frank 46-7
Woodhouse, George 49
Woods, Tiger 84
Wooldridge, Ian 169
Worrell, Frank 63,85
Wright, Doug 75,100

Y
Yardley, Norman 102